The media h**‗‗‗‗‗‗**

reputation

Nobody would dream of going for a job interview without preparing. A lot rides on them and so we prepare. But every day public sector managers find themselves in interviews with journalists with little more than a passing thought. Yet so much more can depend on these events - your reputation, that of your organisation, and more importantly, perceptions about the quality of the services you provide. This book is about helping public sector managers maximise the opportunities that the media present. And it's about minimising the damage that poorly managed relationships can cause.

There's a lot in this book so it might be a good idea to dip in and out.

reputation
52 Newbold Road
Desford
LE9 9GS

The reputation website is www.e-reputation.co.uk

First published 2003

© reputation 2003

Mark Fletcher-Brown asserts the moral right to be identified as the author of this work

Cover image by reputation
Cover design and layout by em communications
Cartoons by Dave Follows

A catalogue record for this book is available from the British Library

ISBN 1-904793-00-2

Printed and bound in Great Britain by
Martins the Printers Ltd, Berwick upon Tweed

Contents

1 Don't panic

A quick survival plan for handling media calls

If you get a call from the media...

Find out what the story is

What's the journalist interested in? Why call you? Do you know anything about it? Get as much information as you can and keep a note.

Establish the deadline

Find out what the deadline is. It's best to know what deadlines your media work to. But ask anyway.

Create some thinking space

Say you're in the middle of something and you'll call them back. Use this time to collect your thoughts, key facts and to focus your attention.

Determine what's in it for you

Weigh it up. Look at the benefits to your organisation in responding. Look at the best and worst case scenarios. Now make a judgement - yes or no.

Think audience, message, outcome

Get the audience into your mind. Be clear about what you want to say to that audience and frame your message for them. Do what you can to link your message to existing plans that relate to that audience.

Stick to the point

Don't allow yourself to be drawn into other questions that you haven't thought through. And certainly don't make it up as you go along. Risk is inversely proportional to preparation.

2 Developing a media strategy

You will get more out of media relations if you plan. It's crucial to be clear about what you are trying to achieve, what is achievable, and the steps you will take to ensure maximum positive and minimum negative coverage.

In all of the interviews I have ever done, those which worked best for me as a journalist were those where the subject did not have a clear idea in advance about what they intended to say to whom and for what purpose.

In other words, unfocused interviews were and are opportunities for journalists.

In the early days of my interviews it did the interviewee no harm because many of the things I should have focused on I missed. Like one director of education who confessed to reading the works of Joseph Stalin before he went to sleep every night. When he was dismissed some months later, and when one of his former colleagues in explaining his early demise described him as a Stalinist, I realised my error. It was not a mistake I was to repeat.

Before you engage in any form of media management you should be clear in your own mind about what you want from that interview. Intelligent people can too easily delude themselves into thinking that they will always get the upper hand in a tussle with a journalist. So rarely is it the case.

To be clear: we all wander around with words and phrases which we use to justify our daily actions but which are rarely tested in any meaningful sense. How many of us talk about *empowering* and *enabling*. Public sector language is full of such prose. But under close scrutiny it rarely stands up.

▲   Empowering whom?

▲ How?

▲ How do you know it worked?

▲ Do those you have empowered want to be so treated?

▲ Did they ask?

▲ When?

▲ In what form?

▲ Where's the evidence?

▲ Do you empower everyone?

▲ On what basis do you distinguish?

And so on.

Journalists, unlike many other people that you will come across in your working life, have a licence to probe. You may decline the opportunity. And that would be your judgement. But the minute the tape is rolling, your reaction to such close inspection could itself become the subject of interest.

So you need to be clear.

But one interview does not a strategy make. This chapter is about how you make the most out of the media opportunities that will face your organisation by creating media strategies.

Let's define some terms here. For the purpose of this book, a strategy is a plan of action which will take you from one place to another. It is different from tactics. Those are the individual actions which bring about one outcome. Tactics may be used as part of a strategy but they are not strategies in themselves. Actions plans are rarely strategies at all since they frequently have no assessment of the starting point and no appraisal of the destination. You just do them.

Before we begin it's worth saying something about the growing interest in *overarching strategies*. It's become a very popular term. It is possible to have an overarching media strategy for your organisation. But the larger the scope of this, the harder it will be to pin down the individual actions that will need to be taken in order to bring about specific outcomes.

In other words, you might not be able to see who will be doing what and with what effect.

Some overarching strategies are no more than statements of intent. You might recognise some of the following phrases:

We will develop a transparent culture
We will seek to build open and honest relationships with the media

These are laudable aims. And if you want to set out some broad principles about how you are going to operate, fine. But make sure that you can connect the general to the specific. Coordinated, connected actions will get you to your destination. Mere words are likely to disappoint.

Or worse, the mere existence of an overarching strategy can give carte blanche to anyone who wants to go their own way - they simply point to your overarching document and claim that their actions fit.

You should seriously consider developing specific media strategies around particular pieces of activity - *we want to build awareness of our health services for local people* - or around particular events.

Developing your strategy should allow you to ask a number of questions. Be clear about the answers before you go on. Taking action because it looks like a good idea may help you solve the problem that you are facing. But it's not a strategy.

What's the outcome?

What are you trying to achieve - is it achievable, have you done it before? Be as specific as possible about this outcome. You may be trying to change behaviour. You may be trying to build awareness of a particular service. You may be trying to keep bad news out of the media altogether. Write this down. You will come back to it throughout the implementation of the strategy.

Challenge yourselves or allow yourselves to be challenged. I have seen many strategies which aim to make the organisation concerned *the best in the country*. Now it's one thing to promote your organisation as the best in the country but the acid test is not the promotion but the actuality.

Equally, you might want your key figures to be known and loved by local people. If so, start with an audit. How are they seen at the moment? Does anyone know who they are or even that they exist?

Remember, a strategy needs a starting point. The more honest you are about the starting point, the more likely you are to find out whether the end point you seek is achievable.

Finally, if you are going to continually improve your media outcomes you need to identify measurables. Look for things that you can measure which will tell you whether you have been successful or not. The phrase "we want a good press" is pretty meaningless, although no less popular for all that. Getting a good press may mean that the bad news that's around your organisation simply doesn't get covered. Or it may mean that you get a significant percentage increase in the number of positive column inches about your organisation in the next period. But be clear. A vague strategy with a non-descript starting point, no clear end-point and little or no evaluation is just activity.

Audiences - who are you talking to?

This is very important. You need to know who you are targeting with your message. The essence of the message may remain the same irrespective of the audience, but the form most certainly won't. And that's because different groups of people see the world in different ways. They have different reference points, use different language, use different concepts to organise the world and have different ways of measuring credibility - you need to know how they judge you and what you might say.

Taking your outcome as a starting point you need to think about the way in which you should frame your message in order to get attention for it and make your message do what you want it to do. If you don't know the audience you are targeting do some research. Don't assume that you know best. Ben Page from MORI once remarked that most newsletters are put together by people who have never talked to anyone outside their organisation, even the people they live with.

Try to capture key words and phrases which are meaningful to each audience. And use these to create your key messages. Understand the problems they face and do what you can to make your messages look and sound like solutions to those problems.

Remember that nobody sees your world as you do. And if you have carried out research for stage one of the strategy you may have established that they don't know the first thing about your organisation. Or that their views are so negative that you will have a lot of work to do before you can even start to promote the positive aspects of your organisation.

Don't forget that most of us in the real world see things through the lens of common sense. If your message doesn't appear to be making sense in common sense terms then it probably won't to most of the people you are talking to. There was a line popular with the government some years ago - *things are getting worse but at a slower rate therefore they are getting better* - which was technically correct. But it never felt that way.

Also, bear in mind that there is a literacy problem in the UK. If you don't take that into account, if you use specialist language, if you need your audience to have prior knowledge before they can engage, they won't.

Finally, remember that you are talking *through* the media. You will have to make what you are saying sufficiently palatable to journalists if you are going to have any chance at all of getting through.

Media - getting your message out

Establish which media your audiences read, see or hear. For most organisations the first port of call will be the local media. Understand them. Get to know the key journalists. Look at the way that they currently handle news. You may, for example, find that your local paper likes to campaign on issues.

The more you know about the media the better. Establish their deadlines. Look at how they are competing with each other and how they are differentiating themselves from competing media.

Be open to all ideas. You don't need to rely upon mainstream media. Parish magazines reach people. As do specialist publications - the trade press. If in doubt, consult one of the media bibles such as *Willings* or *Benn's Media Guide*.

Research the journalists that you will need to talk to. There may well be ambitious young journalists who are keen to make a name for themselves. Use them.

What will you have to do to get your message across?

Often, it's not enough to merely say something if you want to connect with an audience. They will want to see some action. That may be no more than a photo-opportunity - the Chair of the Health and Social Care Portfolio seen walking around the ward with local nurses and doctors for example. But it may be more than that. It will be important here to look beyond the message again to the outcome you are trying to create. One of the reasons for the growth in cynicism about the "spin culture" is that we all know that talk is cheap. Your message is likely to grow in credibility if you are clear about who will need to take which actions in order to create the outcome you want.

It's also going to be important that you use other channels to convince your audiences that you've done what you said you would do. This is where your media strategy should link in with your overall communication strategy. Ideally, the media strategy should be a subset of the latter. The danger here is that you create a media strategy that makes no linkages to other communication, opening up the possibility that you could be *saying one thing and doing another.*

Messages - what will you say to your key audiences?

This is an important part of your media strategy since it is the part where you focus upon the actual words you will use. And for that reason there is a whole chapter devoted to key messages. But there are some rules you will need to bear in mind.

▲ *Repetition equals reality* - the more we hear something, particularly if we hear the same words, the more likely we are to believe it. When you develop key messages make sure that you are consistent in their use.

▲ *Make them talk* - there are mission statements being used up and down the country that don't talk at all. In other words, they are constructed in written language. Sometimes that will be because they are written in the third person - *the trust believes its role to be*. At other times, it's because the words and phrases are never used in day to day conversation.

▲ *Make them talk to the audience* - this means two things. First, put them in a language that the audience will understand. And second, make them address the concerns that your audiences have. The danger here is that your organisation puts together a message which is meaningful *in organisational terms* rather than in terms of key audiences. Think of the benefits to the audience rather than the organisation.

▲ *Make them memorable* - the more your audience can remember, and, at best, repeat your message, the more effective your strategy is likely to be.

Messengers - who is speaking to your key audiences?

Before you select the messenger - the person who will say your key messages (through a press release, in a feature, in a speech, at an event, in a radio interview) - go back to the outcome that you are trying to create. Think about the kinds of qualities that this person should have.

For example:

▲ Do they need to be "important"?

▲ Do they need to be known to the audience?

▲ If they are known, what are they known as, what associations would they create?

▲ What personal qualities should they have? Should they seem stern, strong, sympathetic, personable, caring? And so on.

▲ Do they have the skills?

▲ Who would the audience expect to speak?

This is not an exclusive list. But you should look at it before you start to think about the other factors that might affect your judgement - their position in the organisation, habit, availability.

Spend some time on this area. The messengers should be a part of your overall positioning strategy - the way you represent how you want your organisation to be seen and experienced - so it will be worth looking at the values you want to convey. For example, an acute healthcare trust will want to convey clinical qualities as well managerial competence. Underneath that there will be unspoken qualities such as *caring, efficient, clean* and so on. The individuals you select should *represent* those features too. Put simply: the trust could present a contradictory message if the natural demeanour of your key messengers was efficient rather than caring even though the issue that they were representing had nothing to do with either quality at that time.

What will get in the way of your media strategy?

It's important to build into the strategy all of the factors that could get in the way of success. Some of these will be predictable - people and interests who might seek to hijack your story for their own ends. In this case, you should map out those interests and make a judgement about how you might play the story on the basis of the way that you think they will behave.

You should also look at unpredictable events. Think of possible worst case scenarios, which if they occurred could undermine the success of the strategy. Whereas you can more or less guess where the awkward squad might come from it can be harder to look at these questions. But it needs to be done. This is especially so in high-risk media strategies. For example, you may decide that in order to crack down on public litter in your area you will fine anyone caught dropping it. Here you might want to look at the habits of your own staff since this may well be the first place where the media will go should they want to focus on either the nanny state or hypocrisy at the Town Hall.

In crises, this kind of reputation risk management can be harder since there will always be those who will seek to milk situations for their own ends. Anyone wishing to bring about a change in the status quo can use crises to up the stakes in the story since the media will be looking for someone to take the blame. You can easily find that those who are best informed - those with an inside view of things - can be those who will make the most of such situations.

Resources - how much is it all going to cost and do you have the right resources?

I have seen many communication strategies which make no mention of resources. It's as if the thing will implement itself without anyone having to lift a finger. That's a recipe for disappointment.

There are many management tomes which will tell you all about the art of allocating resources. I won't devote space to that here. You might want to look at *The Effective Executive* by Peter Drucker or *Simply Brilliant* by Fergus O'Connell. Both will help you to find ways of optimising the time you have.

It's worth noting that implementing the most moderate media strategy will eat up time. And unless you have staff with empty diaries, then something will have to give.

But besides time, there are other resource issues to consider.

Skills - you will need to have staff who are able to manage the interface, who understand the way that journalists think and are confident in dealing with them. It's not something that will happen on paper alone. Badly managed media relations, caused by individuals who do not have the appropriate skills, can expose your organisation to additional risk.

Linkages - is everyone within your own organisation who needs to be plugged into your media strategy connected?

Other events - have you taken account of other events or activities that are being planned in other parts of the organisation?

Review - how will you know that it has worked?

The work that you did at the beginning - determining the outcomes - should stand you in good stead here. It's vital that you are honest about whether your strategy delivered the outcomes that you wanted.

It will be important to have *tracking* indicators - items that you can measure during the course of the strategy. These can be reviewed during the strategy as well as at the end. These will provide you with valuable learning points which will help you to improve your next media strategy. But tracking these indicators will also provide you with the opportunity to change course should you find that your strategy isn't turning out as you might have planned it.

Separate those indicators which you feel you ought to have - *we want lots of media coverage* - from those which tell you whether the outcomes you are trying to create are actually happening. And bear in mind that some of the indicators might be invisible. Strategies can be written to keep things out of the media as much as to get things in.

3 Understanding the media management engine

The more visible a message is, the more often it is repeated in credible media, the greater the number of people who will either believe it, or act on it, or both.

The idea is simple. If credible media report nice things about your organisation over time then people will believe it to be true. And the reverse is also true - if credible media report unpleasant things about your organisation then people will tend to believe that to be the case.

This book is about how you promote positive messages about your organisation through the media and minimise the coverage of negative messages.

The problem, though, isn't just whether negative messages get coverage or not. It's that the media can have an important impact on how you and your services are seen by the public. Research by MORI shows that positive and negative coverage can have an impact on the way that people feel about public services in general.

The NHS 50th Anniversary

In the run up to the NHS 50th Anniversary MORI tracked media coverage of the NHS. They also polled to find out whether there was any relationship between the level of coverage and perceptions of service quality.

The first graph shows that awareness of the NHS increased dramatically during the 50th Anniversary week.

The second graph illustrates the point. Perceptions of quality of NHS services remained fairly constant until the week of the 50th Anniversary. At that point, as you will see below, more people reported that they were satisfied with the way that NHS services are run.

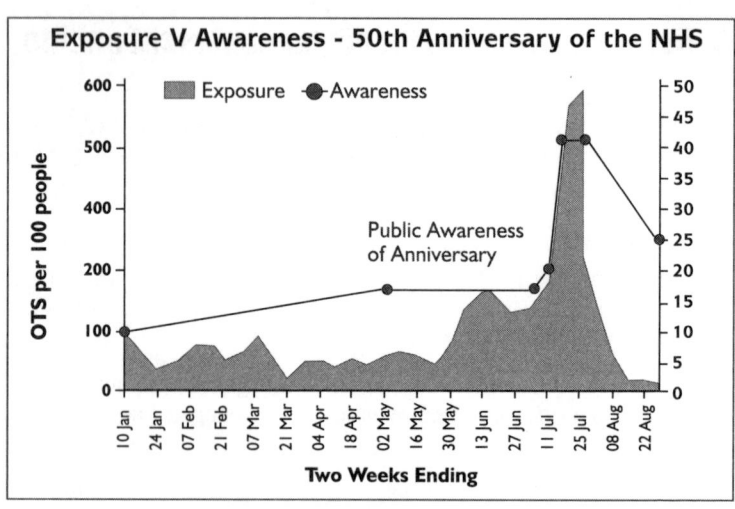

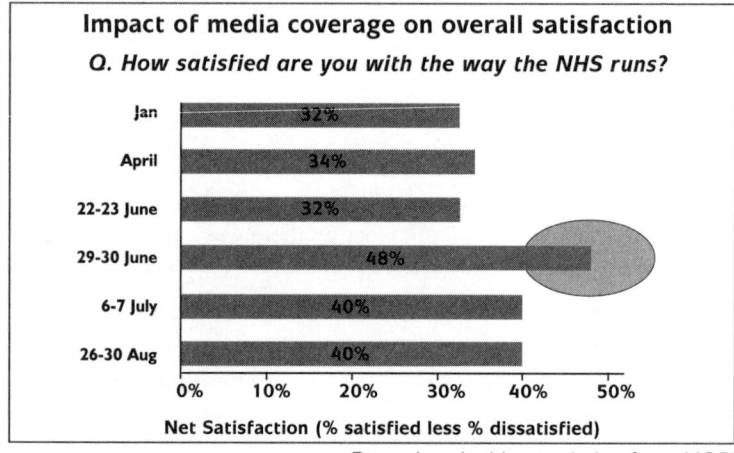

Reproduced with permission from MORI

The shaded area represents media coverage during the week of the anniversary. Interestingly, there is a halo effect. Perceptions after the 50th Anniversary week remained higher than the previous average. In all probability, the reason for the increase in satisfaction will have a great deal to do with simply reminding them that the NHS is a great British institution.

For most people most of the time trying to understand public services, media coverage is all they've got to go on. And therein lies the importance of managing media relationships.

If the only contact that your stakeholders or citizens have with you is through a third party, then that communication could have a disproportionate impact on the way that you are seen.

Gerald Ratner's jewellery was no better or no worse the day after he was reported describing it as "crap". But the net impact of extensive coverage of that remark was enough to wreck his business. People saw him and Ratner's differently.

Heavy communication - factors that will add weight to your message

This section will explain factors that will add weight to positive and negative messages about your organisation and the multiplier effect, ways in which a single repetition of a message can spawn extensive coverage.

Location

If you get coverage in a newspaper, facing, or right-hand pages are more important than non-facing pages. The front page is the most important facing page of all, followed by three, then five and so on. Non-facing pages (2, 4, 6) are less important. In broadcast news, the closer to the top of the bulletin, the more important the news is thought to be. Radio news will also accentuate the significance of a story by adding it into the headlines.

Space

Simply, how much space is a story given? A major story may not only have headlined front page coverage but many other pages given over to new angles or detail or pictures. Broadly, the more space the story is given, the more important it is. In broadcast news, air time is space. More important stories are given more air time.

Position

For newspapers, the most important items will be called "lead" stories. Those are the ones at the top of the page, usually with the boldest or biggest headlines.

It follows that if you have a front page lead story with a number of follow on stories inside then that's going to get the most attention from the readers.

The multiplier effect

In the early 1990s I persuaded the Times Educational Supplement that in this image conscious world they might be interested in a story on image consultancies and whether they ever work with schools. They bought it. And so I set about trying to establish whether schools ever indulged in this kind of activity.

Not only did I discover that they did, but I found out that there were a number of consultancies offering services directly to teachers. The resulting feature was published in the Times Educational Supplement. Within a week it had appeared in a number of other national newspapers. And by the end of the month the image consultants I had spoken to were on breakfast TV.

The multiplier effect is where a single story can spawn the repetition of the same message or story in other media.

Multipliers can be very positive. If your council chief executive has just been voted the most caring public servant in the country, then doubtless there will be coverage locally and elsewhere. But, if your service has been lambasted as the *worst in the nation* by a major public body at a time when the media has an appetite for such things then you could well find yourself at the wrong end of a P45.

Multipliers are not straightforward. Because each media channel will want to make the story relevant to their audience they will look for a new angle on the story.

I don't now remember what other newspapers did with the image consultancy story but you can quickly imagine what they might do with it. One might ask whether image consultancies were making teachers sexier (maybe for a national fashion page) whereas others might ask whether teachers have lost the plot and were relying upon frippery rather than facts to improve schooling (maybe for an education page). TV channels might have looked at makeovers. Or they might have asked leading image experts to advise teachers on how to improve their image. Radio stations might have conducted polls on the best dressed teacher and so on.

The point is that the more the story is repeated, the more it can be unpredictable, with every other journalist trying to use the story to engage *their* readers, listeners or viewers.

Other interests can act as multipliers

It's not just the media that can extend the life of a story. In any environment there are always groups of people or individuals who can piggyback onto a story and milk it for their own ends.

So far as your organisation is concerned this represents another factor in the risk/benefit assessment that you should undertake before you get into an interview.

Let's look at an example:

Mental health patients locked up in Victorian wards

Imagine that following an inspection you had been labelled "the worst mental health trust in the country". Now it might happen that this was stated when there was very little happening news-wise in your area. And as part of making the story real to readers your local paper had highlighted some instances where your practice has been questionable. Again, for the sake of argument, let's say that you had routinely locked patients up for their own safety.

This combination of events could easily turn into:

Worst trust in the country locked up patients in Victorian mental institution scandal

The two lines here that would do you the most damage are:

Worst in the country
Locked up in Victorian mental institution

In terms of the immediate *footprint,* the local newspaper will send out that message to people who are aware of your trust, to those who are not (but will be now), to your patients, to your staff and to your patients' families or carers.

In all likelihood, the story will be picked up by the local radio stations too (and other local papers if you have them).

The same audiences will hear the same thing all over again.

But in a quiet news period it won't necessarily stop there. If there is little else happening nationally at the time - during the summer period (also known as the Silly Season) - then this story could well get many other airings.

National newspapers may want to send journalists to look at the worst mental health wards in the country. They will want to use pictures. They may use library pictures of outdated wards from their files to illustrate the point. They could talk to carers and parents. They could interview former patients who under the right conditions could say all sorts of emotive things - *It was terrible. I lived in fear of the dark, it was then that the demons came. I can still hear their screams now.*

Those two damaging lines will now be seen and heard *yet again* by your local audiences. And now, they're going to be seen and heard by other audiences - local people in other parts of the country, potential users, potential employees, politicians, the department of health.

But here things can get even more complex.

Left to its own devices a story, even where it is repeated, will naturally die. But every story creates a potential opportunity.

Commentators

Let's stay with our fictitious mental health trust for a moment. You've just received this damning report. Others will want to seize the opportunity that this report presents to get their message across.

A number of other interests may be waiting in the wings for a negative story about mental health to push their interests forward, to repeat their lines in a way that leads to new actions, or changes in behaviour.

Look at the following table. It shows how different interests might use a story to make their own point.

Story: Mental health trust condemned

Commentator	Key message
Local patient groups	Management should be sacked
Patients' families	Call for compensation and apology
Local councillors	New management needed at NHS trust, patients let down badly
Local MPs	New campaign called for to rid mental health of last vestiges of Victorian era; more money needed in health services
Government	This is part of our drive to weed out incompetence
Local newspaper	Campaign to close ward and sack management
Mental health charities	This practice is widespread and should be condemned
Special interest groups	Need a change to the law to make care approaches more open to public scrutiny

Every story has the potential to spin out of control, and to keep spinning until it makes someone somewhere take some action. Think about this when you start to plan what might happen to your news.

4 Don't pick up that phone!

Media relations can be very seductive. Being interviewed can give you a sense of importance and significance. But unless you engage with the media on your terms you may expose yourself and your organisation to unnecessary risk.

Are you on or off the record?

Before you get into any interview you should be clear about whether the journalist expects your comments to be on or off the record. Many people are not clear about the difference between the two and can too easily assume that passing remarks, helpful context and informal briefings are off the record whereas the stuff that you say when the tape recorder is running is on the record.

Off the record means that anything you say can be used but *not* attributed.

On the record means that anything you say can be used *and* attributed.

And a good operating assumption is this: if you don't say it's off the record, then it will be treated as if it is on the record.

But since not everyone shares these definitions you should agree the ground rules before the interview starts.

The interview may not start and end where you think

Being clear about on and off the record matters because anything you say *and at any point* - may be quoted. For example, you might invite a journalist to your office for an interview only to find that passing remarks made by members of your staff in the outer office find their way into the copy. Equally, you may be chatting to a journalist after an interview, in the car park, or over coffee, and realise when it's too late that your throwaway comments become the story.

It's worth bearing in mind that John Major's comments about members of his cabinet being "bastards" was actually said to Michael Brunson after the interview but whilst the camera was still running.

It's not dissimilar to *trial by prawn*. In job interviews we pay attention to the way that candidates will comport themselves over lunch. It matters. We believe that it will tell us something about the way that they really are. Journalists use the same technique over coffee to check whether your interview message rings true.

For example, you might choose to meet a journalist over lunch to talk about an impending financial crisis in your organisation and inadvertently order the most expensive thing on the menu and cause him or her to believe either that you are comfortable wasting public money or that you are not serious about saving it.

Set your rules and agree them

You should expect to be able to negotiate some safe territory with local journalists. The reason is that they will need you. If you are a good source of news, or if you are able to get in the way of your organisation providing news, then they will need you. Equally, in order to get your message across to local audiences you will need them - it's a symbiotic relationship.

As a result it may be possible to share briefing material with them that will make their job easier (since it will explain the background to particular issues) and know that it won't go any further.

You won't get this in writing.

The reality is that you will only be able to maintain this relationship whilst you need them and they need you.

Don't pick up that phone!

If your job was under threat (and you therefore became less useful) this arrangement could easily break down. Or if you were sitting on a major story that could leak out through another media channel (with whom you did not have a relationship) or be picked up by another journalist then all bets could quickly be off.

Added to that, you might find that the journalist has his or her own plans. Ambitious journalists will move on - to bigger newspapers, to radio stations, to television, and to bigger salaries. Your scalp may be their passport.

Try to see your relationship in mature terms

It's easy for public service managers to somehow feel aggrieved that their tame journalist has left them twisting in the wind when a story that had been held back somehow found its way on to the front page of the local rag. These things will happen. In reality, and especially because of the increasing neurosis about spin, media channels are forced to establish their independence of public organisations.

The more they appear to be tame to their readers/viewers/listeners, the less they can be helpful to you. If their readers, viewers or listeners believe that the media are somehow part of the spin machine - there to convey official propaganda - then their position in the market place will be threatened. And worse, from your point of view, they will not be able to convey *your* messages when you need them to. There's little or no point in getting your story into a publication that makes it no further than the cat litter tray, or onto a radio station that is no more than afternoon wallpaper.

The relationship that your organisation is able to have with journalists will be at its best if you are both able to understand each other's position.

Get personal

Take symbiosis to its logical conclusion. Helping a journalist to get copy is a good start. If you can make them look good, by ensuring that they are onto the stories that matter, if their facts are accurate and if their reports are timely, then you will be helping them.

But your help can go a lot further. The more you know about where your media contacts see their career the better. You may find that you have a future Paxman on the staff of the local *Daily Bugle*. He or she will know that they won't get where they want to be going by being nice to people all of the time. You will need to know that.

Ambitious journalists who don't see themselves as people who will be hanging around in *Nowheresville* for the rest of their lives will probably not mind too much about upsetting a few people en route. Even so, they will probably have some special interests and you may be able to help them by getting them access to key facts and figures more easily.

Equally, other journalists may see themselves as a part of the local area. Not everyone moves around the country chasing big jobs. Those who are here for a while will still need to look good. Aware of the pressure inside their organisation, the continuous pressure to produce more, the constant squeeze on resources (given the shrinking market) and the young hopefuls nipping at their heels, they may want to be part of relationships which keep them well-fed.

Remember, it's business

In other words, it's not personal. Journalists, like the police, can't hear things that they feel they ought to report and do nothing about it. If you inadvertently blurt out something very newsworthy in front of your local hack then unless you are married to this person, expect it to find its way into the public domain. Journalists feel the urge to share your mistakes with the world.

And it's an income stream

Local journalists can turn your news into a better income by simply passing on your story to the nationals. In return for good news leads national papers will pay local sources.

Share it

You may feel that your relationships with journalists are personal. But you will increase the risk to your organisation of unmanaged media relations if you don't share information about the way that journalists are as individuals. Journalists will want to foster personal relationships. It's their way of getting through to people when it matters.

Have you caused the call?

Public bodies are in the unique position in British life of having to air just about every significant decision before, during and after it is made. A journalist may have called you because you have published documentation that has attracted their interest. Ideally, before you send something out into the public domain you should have some idea about the impact it's likely to cause.

Has someone else caused the call?

Have you sent out a press release? If so, get a copy of it. Make sure that your own protocols ensure that if you should know about public statements you do. Don't allow yourself to inadvertently blunder into remarks made by someone else.

Equally, when you produce public papers you should ensure that media risks (and opportunities) are assessed before the papers go live *and that everyone who should know about this does*.

What's in it for you?

Don't be seduced into an interview because it seems like a good idea. Have a clear notion of the benefits to you or your organisation. Crucially, how will talking to this audience help you to achieve your key goals? It may be that you want to use the conversation to keep a dialogue open with the journalist. If so, fine. But if you can't see a benefit then seriously question whether you ought to take the call.

▲ Are you clear about the benefit to either you or your organisation?

▲ Are you clear about the risks of not speaking?

▲ Are you sufficiently in control of your message to be able to deal with the interview?

▲ Do you have a clear message?

▲ Do you know how to get into and out of the interview?

Tactics

On specific issues, you need to be clear about how you will manage the delivery of your key messages without exposing yourself to the risk of other things coming out that you don't want to talk about. This needs skill, control, experience and a proper examination (particularly on complex issues) of the routes into and out of the interview before you start. As airline pilots say, it's a lot easier to sort out problems on the ground before you take off.

5   Journalists - an audience you need to know and understand

They're not monsters - just people trying to do a job.

Lots of people are frightened of journalists. Their public image is one which would inspire fear - they bring careers down, they expose weakness, they harangue, question and challenge important people. They are given licence by their readers and viewers to get to the heart of the matter. And our image of journalists is mostly fed by leading protagonists - the likes of James Naughtie, Lynn Barber, Kate Adie, John Humphrys and Jeremy Paxman.

The reality is this: any message you want to get across to outside audiences (as opposed to your staff) will have to go through journalists so you need to both understand them and be comfortable with them.

Here are some things you will need to bear in mind when you build relationships with journalists.

They're focused

There is little time to waste. If you are in any doubt about this make a visit to your local newspaper office. You will find an atmosphere that borders on the frantic at times. People rushing about trying to get things written and finished in time for the next edition.

What does this mean to you?

You need to know what you want to say when you speak to them. They will know what they want when they speak to you. If you are not clear you will expose yourself to unnecessary risk.

They must be predatory

A leading journalist once told me a story which captured the predatory nature of their trade. As a trainee he started on a local newspaper and was sent off to write a story. After half an hour wandering round the office looking for a typewriter he went back to the editor to report that he couldn't find one. He was given short shrift and told to go off and find one. The solution was to go to the desk of an absent colleague and steal his. It was a lesson that stood him in good stead.

The driver is simple: he or she who takes, gets. That driver will sort out those who will go out and find the contacts, get the stories and meet the deadlines from those who won't last long.

They deliver or they die

The media doesn't carry passengers. Journalists' work is scrutinised daily by consumers and editors alike. Those who don't deliver don't survive.

They will expect you to be evasive

It is not the age of spin that has made journalists wary of organisations that manage their news. It's common sense. Everyone has something to hide. Any organisation or group of people that does anything at all will have made mistakes. Everyone knows this. And nobody wants to share their mistakes with anyone else. We all like to present to the world a better version of events than the facts would allow. A journalist will expect you to equivocate.

But it's worse in public services. When a private sector company makes a mistake it only matters to their customers, shareholders and those who are directly affected. When public services make mistakes it matters to everyone - because everyone pays tax.

They will want to keep *those in power under scrutiny* - there is still a sense that journalists wield the sword of truth. They will be seeking to scrutinise your executive and ask the kinds of questions that they believe local people would want answered.

Journalists - an audience you need to know and understand

They are highly motivated

Journalists are driven people. Journalists are focused on *now*. *Now* is when their newspaper comes out. *Now* is the information that will fill it - *then* is history. *Now* drives the production process - be it for newspapers, radio or TV - it has to happen today (or in the case of weekly papers, this week).

In order to survive and to thrive in a now-driven industry, journalists have to be able to go out and find the stories that will fill the pages or the air-time.

To get a feel for this, imagine that every morning the first thing you did when you walked into the office was to look at acres of blank pages. Or you had to give a presentation at 12 noon and you hadn't yet started it. That's what meets journalists, more or less, every day. Yes, they will have done some of the work in advance (newspapers do what are called "overnight pages" and radio and television can prepare packages before broadcast date). But the desire for newly harvested news, and the need to fill pages with that, means that your average journalist begins work with a heavy stress load.

They are competitive

One of the ways in which a journalist will motivate him or herself is with the realisation that they won't be the only person chasing the news. They will be competing with journalists from other media channels for the same stories. And they may be competing with other journalists from their own newspaper, radio station or TV programme.

In *Diary of a tabloid journalist*, Wesley Clarkson talks about the pressure on journalists to go out and get the story, to be first, to get there before the opposition do. Getting an exclusive on a story can add thousands of extra copies to the daily sales. Neither are many of the challenges that journalists face in getting the story particularly pleasant. A local news editor may want pictures of the victims following a fatal car crash. Well, you can't ask the victim so a journalist will have to ask the family. That means going to a relative's door in the wake of a bereavement and asking them for pictures of loved ones. And getting there before any of your competitors do. That's no mean task. On top of that, some journalists will talk about gathering all of the pictures so that when the opposition do get there, there will be no spoils to be had.

Competition inside a newspaper or radio station can be equally fierce. If competition is one of the drivers, then the ability to compete and win can be one of the key marks of a star.

They are semi-autonomous

Journalists may not have much power in terms of control over budgets or many staff. Few in regional papers will have more than an assistant. And they may even struggle to get their expenses claims paid. But they do have the ability to take a simple slip up and turn it into a national story. Even those who work in free weeklies can do that. They will seek to publish without fear or favour.

In order to preserve their sense of independence, journalists will have their own sources which they will guard jealously, their own ways of working, their own patches and a clear sense of the need to stay away from vested interests. They will dislike spin or any form of manipulation.

They are not all well-paid

You might even say that for the majority of journalists that public sector managers will come across, most are poorly paid. Such is the continued desire of people to join the media that there is a downward pressure on salaries - pay for most is not getting better.

A journalist working for a free weekly paper (those full of advertising distributed free to our homes) could be earning between £7,000 and £12,000 a year. Even successful daily journalists on regional papers can be earning anywhere between £18,000 and £30,000 a year. Journalists on national papers will earn more. But national newspapers are fiercely competitive. If you don't deliver then you won't last long. Added to that, nationals still use short term contracts, freelancers and day and night shifts to keep the media machine working.

The system persists because commercial organisations keen to maximise their profits (or to minimise their costs) will keep salaries down. And the demand from fresh faced graduates for jobs in the media remains high.

And so far as performance is concerned, when you talk to people inside the media they report human resources practices which are quite different to public sector processes. Poor performers are more likely to be sat down with their manager and a cheque book - *tell me how much I should put in this box then you can leave* - rather than endless performance reviews, structural changes and special projects.

The effect of a *sink or swim culture* (coupled with the realisation that there are millions of communication studies degree students ready and willing to take your place) is high performance. Slackers will fall by the wayside.

Success is delivery, delivery, delivery

Many of the *names* in journalism began life in humble places. Most national stars will have started their career in local papers or in local radio. These are the stamping grounds as well as the training grounds. Time-serving is not the route to a better career. People don't get moved up because they've been there a long time. Rather, those who will move from local free weeklies to regional dailies to nationals or from local commercial radio to the BBC and beyond are those who deliver what the editor wants time and time again.

And more, they will second guess what he or she wants and then deliver what they were going to want.

They can't help it

Like the police (who are sworn officers of the law 24 hours a day) journalists don't switch off. A passing remark, over a drink at the weekend, will be logged and may return in a story at some point.

6 Thinking like a journalist

We all think like journalists. But we don't do it all the time. Every time we pick up a paper or listen to a news broadcast, we reconfirm that way of thinking. News is a manufactured product. It takes the complexity of daily life and reduces it into a digestible form that we recognise as *news*. We know news when we hear it.

The real truth is very complex.

It's about telling stories and how you tell them

Journalists tell us stories. Stories have plots and main characters. We know the stories before they are written. The names and places will change but we are all pretty good at predicting what will happen in the stories that we are told.

Certain stories never get an airing. For example, there is limited space available for good news stories, something which is occasionally lamented by journalists themselves. It's not the journalists fault - we, the consumers, are really not all that interested in endless tales telling us how well organisations and people are doing. *Hospital staff kind says new survey*. Really? That's probably only interesting to those staff, their families and to the chief executive.

Whereas bad news stories - *nurse slapped me says 92 year old patient* - is instantly fascinating to us all.

It's easy to get lost in the academic debate about the nature of news stories, so don't. To get a feel for the way in which we will all find the strongest way into a story look at the following four events:

- ▲ Former hospital chief executive to be charged over expenses fraud

- ▲ Three die in a ferry disaster in Italy

- ▲ Council plans to close community centre have been leaked

▲   Man wins the pools but discovers his coupon was not submitted by the agent

Over the last five years, these stories have been used as a training aid in media relations for public sector managers, staff and councillors throughout the UK. When asked to find the strongest angle on these stories the following, almost without exception, happens.

Former hospital chief executive to be charged over expenses fraud

Strong angle

This is always seen to be a man and delegates focus on his extravagant lifestyle and "commission" pictures of his luxurious mansion, expensive car and attractive companion. They want library shots of him taking a charity cheque which would by implication make it look like he was taking a bribe.

Stories

How the mighty are fallen; you can't trust people where money is concerned - they'll always let you down; men simply can't be trusted.

It never matters that the fraud is as yet unproven and may have nothing to do with his or her present work.

Three die in a ferry disaster in Italy

Strong angle

These people are either young - cut off in their prime - or on the holiday of a lifetime. They are pillars of the community or young people with their whole life ahead of them. Delegates always want pictures of them, interviews with grieving relatives and comments which show how much their whole community will miss them. Occasionally, delegates blame the ferry company.

Stories

Young lives cut short; a community grieves; you can't trust foreign ferries.

Delegates rarely discuss whether the deceased were to blame in any way, whether there may have been foul play or whether alcohol may have been a factor. And whether or not they were known, let alone loved, by their communities is irrelevant.

Council plans to close community centre have been leaked

Strong angle

The council is letting the community down, again. The emphasis is always on the impact of that decision. Delegates want pictures of people looking distraught holding placards. They always focus on what it will mean to vulnerable people.

Stories

The council will always let you down; the paper will fight for the community (by running a campaign to keep it open).

Man wins the pools but discovers his coupon was not submitted by the agent

Strong angle

A working class man in his fifties who lives on a council housing estate and might have used the money either to have a holiday of a lifetime or to pay for his disabled daughter to have a life-saving operation has been cheated out of a fortune. The pictures always show him distraught in poorly made clothes in poverty-stricken surroundings.

Stories

The poor always get cheated.

The man is always hard up and if you suggest that he may be a wealthy businessman who does the pools out of habit then none of the delegates (posing as media people) are ever interested.

Thinking like a journalist

The quickest way to prepare yourself to make the most out of the media is to learn to think like a journalist. Every day, public sector managers allow stories to get out into the media in ways which damage the reputation of their services because they don't allow themselves to see their news as their audience would.

The challenge is to be able to look at your services from the point of view of your main audience. In most cases, that will be local people. That's what journalists do.

● **What's going to make the biggest difference to the lives of your audience?**

Think about what you're doing in terms of the impact that it might have on the lives of your key audiences. You may be delivering a service - but to your audience what matters is how what you do impacts on their lives. When journalists make news real they will look at what people can or can't do as a result of what has happened. A cut in hospital services, for example, might mean that people will die.

You need to see your services in terms of the impact that they will have. The bigger the impact, the more important the news.

● **What kind of story is it?**

It might be argued that we read, see or hear the same stories day in day out. All that happens is that the names and faces change. Certainly, the media present a selective version of reality - it's a *represented* reality.

In the *represented* world, big things happen all the time. Most people don't get killed on the road, get murdered in their beds, get abducted, get involved in sex scandals, win the lottery against the odds or get reunited with long lost brothers or sisters as they lie on their death beds.

Now this is not a criticism. The truth is that to most of us, day to day life, the normal world, is not something we would want to read about. That's what we live. But we want to read about the dramatic stuff - it's the material that confirms our worst fears and suspicions.

Begin by looking at what you do, what you've done and what you might do and understand whether it falls into the category of the unusual, interesting and "it could happen to me".

● **Think of the stereotypes**

Added to that, there are key stereotypes running through journalism. Think about your daily news diet. In the journo-world:

▲ Public services are faceless organisations that do things to people, often with scant regard for their feelings

▲ They make decisions behind closed doors and when they consult they've already made up their minds

▲ When they make mistakes they're unlikely to admit to it - rather they'll go all out to cover it up

▲ They will be prone to spending public money unwisely

▲ Real people are the victims rather than the beneficiaries of their decisions

▲ Managers in these organisations live in a *one rule for me, another rule for you world*. This hypocrisy is best found in the way that they spend our money - pay hikes, over-blown expenses, executive cars, free car parking spaces, subsidised lifestyles, junkets.

You need to understand whether your news confirms these and other stereotypes.

Putting your journalist thinking-cap on at work

Unless you are about to change career, it's unlikely that you'll have to think like a journalist. But it will help you if you can anticipate the way they might think.

Some questions you might want to ask.

- ▲ What are the key facts - what makes it really interesting?
- ▲ What would I want to tell other people?
- ▲ What would I want to say in the pub on a Friday night about this?
- ▲ How would I illustrate the essence of the story?
- ▲ What facts capture it for me?
- ▲ What comment sums it up?

7 Selling your stories to the media

Getting media coverage on any terms is not difficult. Getting media coverage on your own terms is more tricky. Here are some tips to help you pick up free space.

Sell people

Understand the kinds of stories that the media you contact would want to write or run anyway. Broadly, it's people not processes that sell. And the people they will be interested in are their own consumers and their lives.

So think about your services in terms of the impact that they have on real people and frame your story ideas in those terms to journalists. For example, you may be consulting local people on the kinds of services they might want you to run. Consultation processes are not interesting. But what could happen as a result of the consultation to people in their communities might be. So paint pictures for the media and help them find people-driven ways into the story.

If you must focus on process - sometimes you will not want to set hares running by speculating about what might happen - make that interesting. You could focus on particularly interesting ways of being consulted (meeting with firemen by their poles, going out on lifeboats with rescue crews and so on). Those are ways in which *people* can be seen to be a key part of the story.

Sell at the right time

Journalists are busy people. And the busiest times of the day will be the deadlines they work to. Find out when those deadlines are and ensure that you don't phone as the deadline approaches. You will get short shrift.

Sell what they already buy

Before you try to sell anything at all, look at what already gets coverage in the media you are interested in. For a start, you are more likely to get journalists interested in what you've got to say if you can speak with some knowledge about what they've already done. And you know that such stories already interest them.

Cut to the chase

You are likely to find, at least until journalists know that talking to you is going to yield a story, that you are only going to get time on the phone. So you've got to make it count. Don't beat around the bush. And certainly don't try to be too clever - *I've got the kind of story that will make your hair stand on end*. The chances are that you won't have. So you'll begin your relationship with a big let-down. It's best to be tentative but clear. Remember that they are very busy. And they'll be listening out for the spin-angle - they will be thinking: *why is this person telling me this - what have they got to hide?*

Look at how they use your ideas

When you've sold an idea for a story to a journalist check out how it's used afterwards. That will give you clues on their approach. It will also give you something to talk about the next time you call them with a new idea.

Build your relationship and get face to face

As you put ideas forward and gradually find that they get used, this will create confidence both in your own ability to spot good stories and confidence in the journalist. So keep an eye on what happens to your ideas. Look at how they've been adopted or adapted. And take the time to call the relevant journalist to follow things up. You might want to let them know that you've seen their pieces and what you think of them (provided these comments are positive - criticising coverage, especially as an informed reader, is not likely to help you to build a relationship).

Selling your stories to the media

If a journalist sees you as a value-added contact, someone who will feed ideas, stories and contacts, then they'll be keen to get face to face. You still won't be able to let your guard down. But you can keep it up in a less obtrusive way. Remember that although you will be becoming increasingly useful you're still potentially a story that needs to be written.

Make sure that every time you meet with a journalist you give them something that can be turned into something useful - a contact, a story or a lead.

Think ahead

Journalists need to keep abreast of the news, developments, trends and so on. Do some thinking ahead. If you're pitching to their future markets (where they and their editors think they ought to be going) then you could be helping them by giving them leads and useful ideas. Features editors sometimes have future features lists and they will, if you ask them nicely, send these to you.

Understand their woes

Life is tough in the media business. Contracting market share, increased competition, and squeezes on journalists' time and money, mean that life is harder than ever. The Internet is having an impact. Falling sales of regional papers will impact on salaries. The proliferation of the media and its impact on advertising revenue all eat into the stability of their world. Keep that in mind when you speak to them.

Think about the art of influence

There will be hardly a manager in the country who doesn't do this every week. The art of influence relies to a large extent in being able to work out what drives the person whom you are trying to influence. You need to know what they want and what they are doing to get it. And you need to be able to see how you might fit into that equation.

The rules are no different with journalists. The more you understand who they are and what they want the more you are likely to be able to influence them. But you must be careful. Independence is a key part of the journalistic brand so invisibility can be your greatest asset. Just as senior staff might work with board members or councillors behind the scenes and secure influence as a result knowing that the relationship hinges on discretion, so you must behave with the media. Journalists will protect their sources. No-one need ever know that the ideas which generated endless front pages actually came from brown envelopes supplied by you. So much in life depends upon allowing other people to appear to be what they may not be.

Think about the stories they could write

I came across one story that looked like a sure-fire item which turned into a major disaster. An arts officer went to Brazil in a trip funded by an overseas government to find out more about street theatre. The arts officer's employer, a council, spent virtually no money on the trip. The arts officer mentioned this wonderful trip to a news editor over lunch one day thinking it would generate lots of positive coverage. And it might have. But the news editor could see a better story. And it was asking why a cash-strapped council could afford to send a member of staff half way across the world to learn virtually nothing. Or at least that's how it was written.

But it got worse. Following the front page splash that the story yielded, a national tabloid became interested (a local journalist sold it to them) and wrote a more damning story still - *a council arts officer flew to Brazil to watch street actors dance in their underpants*.

When you are selling your stories to the media, keep in mind that the journalist will be thinking of a better angle. Remember, that we all buy conflict - and journalists are always on the lookout for it.

Keep it simple

A final plea for plain talking. You may have the best ideas in the world but lose attention for your story ideas because you are either trying to impress, trying to baffle, trying talk down or just not trying. Think about your audience. Journalists are busy, plain-speaking people. Don't fire off jargon and expect them to be interested. Just keep it straight and you'll be fine.

Six ways to sell your stories

▲ Press releases

▲ Briefings

▲ Press conferences

▲ Passing conversations

▲ Leaks

▲ Brown envelopes

8 Spin!

In media management terms spin means getting journalists to report your news in ways that benefit rather than damage your reputation. Or to keep it out altogether.

Let's be honest here: who has never talked around a subject, missed bits out, emphasised some parts of our story more than others or timed the message just right to present ourselves in a better light?

The short answer: nobody. And that's the essence of spin.

Spin is not, and should never be, lying. It's presenting information in ways which cause people to feel differently about it. It's no different to what barristers do in court, except they're much better at it. And it's exactly what we do every day when we talk to colleagues, friends and family.

Spin is about allowing people to see the side of the story that you want them to see. And because that side is in your interest. There are many ways into any story. What journalists will do is look for the side that is most interesting to their readers, listeners or viewers. Spin is about understanding the routes that journalists will want to take into a story and offering them a nicer path - the route that suits you.

Journalists spin too

Journalists present information in ways that allow us to reach the conclusions they favour.

Take this story. A chief executive of a national public sector agency says in a speech to local authority delegates at a conference that they ought to work harder in engaging central government. His message is subtle. He's not condemning what they've done so far although he does say in one passage:

Spin!

"The truth is that Ministers need to be reminded that you're there. And that's what it's like in government - it's easy to slip off the radar screen."

It all looks very innocuous.

But look at what a journalist might do to it.

TOP BOSS SLAMS LAZY COUNCIL MANAGERS

A top government agency boss today slammed local government managers for allowing councils to "slip off the government radar screen".

And then the journalist might go and ask some delegates what they think about being slammed by this agency boss. One might say: "it's all very well for him, he's paid to talk to government, I'm paid to run council services".

That comment will allow the journalist to justify an angry rebuttal paragraph.

His comments sparked a fierce row with delegates many of whom are angry with the remarks. One dismissed the speech saying that council managers need to concentrate on running council services.

"It's all very well for him, he's paid to talk to government, I'm paid to run council services."

What this approach demonstrates is the ability to *focus* on the strongest angle and then to *add weight* by finding people who will react to that angle.

Of course, this raises some very interesting questions. What was written wasn't what was said - but was it what the speaker wanted to be reported? Was the speaker *coding* his comments to sound inoffensive to the audience present knowing that it would go national anyway? Was the speaker naive?

Daily spin

To get a feel for the reality of daily spin let's look at another story.

Your organisation has decided to reduce a budget which will mean closing down a facility used by a local community.

You can easily imagine the reasons behind this. Let's put some imaginary "facts" on the table.

- ▲ *We are reducing our budget because we have overspent in another area - making these cuts allows us to disguise our ineptitude*

- ▲ *We are cutting these services because it will cause less of a furore than if we had cut others where the recipients are more vociferous*

- ▲ *We are cutting these services because it is not in a politically sensitive area*

- ▲ *We are cutting these services now because it's coming up to national budget time and we don't think anyone will notice*

Anyone who has spent any time in public services will know that these are all possible reasons. But, of course, only a fool would admit to those in public. Rather, we will dress things up so that we put ourselves in a better light. When we do that we spin. We manage the way we represent things to suppress some reasons and to accentuate others.

Practical spin

There are two main reasons behind spin - to make your way of seeing things more attractive to journalists or to make the way they are already seeing things less attractive. In other words, it's about maximising good news and minimising bad news.

Spin works because journalists will tend to simplify stories in order to get them across quickly. They are also under time pressures which makes it necessary for them to take pre-digested information. What's more, the lack of time makes it harder for them to scrutinise and challenge what they are being told.

Here are some of the techniques.

Emphasis

This will be where *the facts of the story* are known, but you are able to put emphasis on certain facts rather than others. This can work because journalists will want to simplify a story in order to get it across. Your pitch here is to emphasise the facts that suit you. There may be any number of reasons behind a decision - this is about emphasising those that allow you to be seen in a particular way.

How to do it: put the facts you want to emphasise at the top of or in a key part of your opening statements.

Attribution

This is about assigning motives to your actions. It's not far from deception since unless the motives you attribute are actually those which you assigned then you are technically not telling the whole truth. Of course, life is not that simple and your attribution may be partly true - you may have had several motives and all you have done is emphasise one more than the others.

How to do it: be careful where you use the word "because". Or don't use it.

It's about implication by juxtaposition. E.g. "We are closing this building. The demand for its use has decreased".

Suggestion or expected inference

This is about presenting facts to a journalist and allowing them to draw their own conclusions. It will work if you firstly control the amount of time you make available, if you take away the opportunity for your statement to be closely scrutinised or if you so emphasise certain facts that the listener can only draw a limited number of conclusions.

How to do it: limit the number of facts to those which convey the message you want.

Saleability

This is allowing people to believe what they would want to believe. It plays on existing prejudices. This works by looking at what the journalist would want to believe and then giving them the facts or opinions that allow them to make the leap. Propositions become saleable because the information will help them to do what they want to do. Journalists will want to fill space with interesting material that matters to their audience in dramatic and engaging ways.

How to do it: think about how a journalist would want to write a particular story.

The law of salient points

This means presenting facts in a way that enables people to *read* a story. The reality is that we will draw conclusions from a limited number of facts that may not represent what the facts may otherwise tell us. And we do this because it is easier. What we are saying is that these are the key facts. And that statement, left unchallenged, will cause the audience to make certain conclusions.

How to do it: think carefully about the route into and through your story and limit time for challenge or clarification.

The law of killer facts

This is where the key facts in the story are so strong that the audience will find it hard to conclude anything but the line that you want to convey. For example, there was a recent media story on school meals which said that the average prisoner's meal costs around 75p whereas the average school meal is just half that. We will naturally conclude that this was grossly unfair. It works because it's simple, easy to digest (as it were) and easy to remember. But if it were to be examined more closely we would have to look at all sorts of other elements of the cost.

How to do it: spend time on strong killer facts.

The law of limited space

Some people have tried to keep things out of the media by choosing a time to release information when there is already pressure on news space.

The law of local trading

Local journalists need local managers. They are their sources of news. They keep the copy flowing and can be relied upon to help fill spaces when there are yawning gaps in the paper or programme. This symbiotic relationship can be exploited by managers when bad news comes along. Basically, it means *obliging* journalists to put less emphasis on a particular story line to preserve *this good working relationship*. The journalist is called upon to make a judgement - will they need this person in the future or can they get away with running this story and still retain the source? Of course, there may come a time when you are less useful to them in which case this law breaks down. The minute you hear a journalist say that they are thinking of moving on, beware.

How to do it: build strong interpersonal relationships with journalists.

The law of the iceberg

Inevitably in public services, some information will have to be confidential. The whole of health is practically kept locked up on the back of patient confidentiality. This law is about suggesting that stuff below the surface is of such significance that it prevents the organisation making a statement about it. The only place to really test this is in open court. And practically, that's not an option.

How to do it: know what you can and can't say and use this sparingly; clarify and maintain your policy on confidentiality.

Timing

This is about managing the release of your information in ways which either maximise interest (giving journalists plenty of time to see copy in advance, providing additional briefing, pitching for the biggest circulation/exposure days) or minimise it (no advance information, little time to prepare prior to deadline.

How to do it: be aware of the deadlines for all of the media that matter.

Leaks

Leaking can be very powerful since the mere act of doing so ascribes certain meaning to the information. It allows the audience to read *the truth* or *stuff they didn't want you to know*. What's more, if your public position is *we don't comment on leaked reports* it allows the organisation to reap the benefits of having the information in the public domain without having to worry about the need to contextualise it.

How to do it: brown enveloped material to journalists; speak loudly in their presence; pass your information to those who like to gossip.

The law of better tales to tell

This is about persuading a journalist determined to write one story (which may disadvantage you) that another is more interesting. A journalist may call you with questions about a story. You may be less cooperative on this story - in meetings, unable to get the information they need - but more so on another story - prepared to give them access to key people, straightforward facts, good pictures. With a space to fill, they may go for the quick win.

How to do it: keep a list of alternative stories that can be wheeled out when needed.

This'll put you in solid with your boss

This means understanding the pressures that journalists are under - they need to have strong sources who will provide them with interesting stories and make their paper or programme look good. In other words, the more you can make them look good, the better they will treat your organisation.

How to do it: think about how the programme or paper is positioning itself and build productive relationships with journalists.

Things that are attractive to journalists...

- ▲ Simple stories involving their key audiences
- ▲ Active language
- ▲ Well-written well-delivered quotable quotes
- ▲ Interesting people
- ▲ Scandal
- ▲ The fall of great people
- ▲ Hypocrisy

...things that are less attractive to journalists

- ▲ Boring text
- ▲ Jargon
- ▲ Process
- ▲ No reference to people
- ▲ Long boring quotes
- ▲ Self-aggrandisement

The spin about spin

The truth about spin is that it's very difficult to tell any story absolutely straight. Every version is a representation. Where you decide to start a story, how you explain it, how you select the main characters, the words you use to describe them, the tone of your voice when you tell it, the pace of your comments, the place you decide to end and the way you react to questions about it all have an impact on the way that an audience will read it. Further, take exactly the same form of words and put them to a different audience and the meaning will change again.

Added to that, we would quickly lose faith in our public institutions if we saw the reality of the decisions that took place behind the scenes. Not everything is planned. Some things are planned but for the wrong reasons. Expediency delivers useful outcomes. Opportunism and personal gain are motivators for change. And so on. If that's the reality of your organisation, how would exposing that reality to your key audiences help you in any way?

In one sense, everything is spin.

9 Key messages and quotable quotes

A brilliant sound-bite can do everything from rallying a nation to changing the way we feel about an issue or a person. But like all excellent text they require enormous talent, extensive preparation, or both.

A key message is something you say to a particular audience in order to bring about a particular outcome. That might mean building awareness, inviting people to take action or just telling them what you think.

You've probably heard people talking about *getting key messages across*. This chapter will explain what that means and how you can create messages which will help to get your and your services message across.

What's behind it all?

The idea is quite simple: if you say the same thing over and over again to the same people in the same way they will eventually believe you provided that their own experience does not in any way conflict with that.

That's the principle. The practice is slightly more complicated but not complex.

For you it means one simple question:

What do you want to say to whom and for what purpose?

Every single manager in the country will know the answer to this question for most of the work that they do. Any council chief executive, for example, will know just how to put his or her proposals to the leader of the council in a way that will get the kind of buy-in they are looking for. And they will know that it's not just how it's said, but also where and when, as well as who should say it. Equally, every doctor will know the right way to put things to his or her patient.

Successful communication depends upon *putting things the right way*. That means sensitivity to the other person. It means thinking about the right words to use. It's about timing. And it's about thinking emotionally.

And it's no different when you are talking to journalists. But there is one added complexity - you talk through journalists to get to other audiences. You therefore need to take account of the needs of all of the groups you might be communicating with.

In this chapter we will look at five specific areas:

▲ Engaging journalists

▲ Finding the right words

▲ Making yourself quotable

▲ Making your words speak

▲ Same words, different mouths - making it all fit together

I Engaging journalists

It is vital if you are going to be able to use the media that you understand the way that journalists will consume your message. There are two main reasons. First, you need to ensure that you convey the point you want to get across as quickly and effectively as possible. Second, you will want to ensure that you don't expose yourself to risk by causing the journalist to focus on things you haven't thought through.

Get to the point
Journalists are time-sensitive. Deadlines and other pressures keep them focused on the task in hand. And like all audiences short of time they need you to get to the point quickly. Don't wander round painting in the context, filling in the background and explaining the footnotes. Get to what you have to say right away. That will make everyone's life easier.

Keep it simple

The simpler you can make your message, the better. Don't dress up the obvious. Try to say what you mean. It's easy to get into jargon. For example, *we fully intend to engage staff in matters about the future structure of the organisation* is simply *we're talking to staff about how things are going to be organised here.*

What journalists will be interested in is what you are doing and what difference it will make. They are interested in actions and outcomes.

But in your simplicity do not lose sight of *what you are actually doing.* It may sound simple to say - *we are setting up a strategic partnership to deliver better healthcare* - but that is a simple way of putting something quite complicated. It's not that easy to understand. It's better to say - *We, in the primary care trust, are working with the local hospital to help improve the health of local people.* Even that may be a long way from what journalists would want. But it's a step in the right direction.

Make it *now*

Focus on what you are doing today or in the near future. Make your comments as definite as possible. Think of the questions that would arise in your own mind if someone said to you, "we will be improving services in the future". You would probably ask: *what will you do, when and what difference will it make?*

Remember, journalists will be writing about your plans for their audiences and they need to be able to answer the questions that others will ask of them.

Tell them what you are doing for the audience they are interested in

Everything a journalist will write will be of interest to their audience. A local paper will not be interested in a national story unless it has local relevance. Remind yourself of the kinds of things that will interest key audiences in the chapter on news values. Don't lose sight of the fact that if they're spending time listening to you ramble on about nothing in particular they're not able to listen to someone else who may have something much more interesting to say.

Get into the habit of reading your local newspapers, listening to local radio broadcasts and watching local TV news.

Solve their problems

Put yourself in their shoes - every day they come to work they've got to fill a huge yawning void. The first problem they have is to have something interesting to write about. If every call you make to a journalist helps them solve that problem your voice will be a welcome sound.

II Finding the right words

Use the words your audiences use

This is the most obvious thing of all but it's one of the things that senior managers can struggle the most with. And that has probably got something to do with the way that we, as people, define ourselves. If you see yourself as an intellectual person you might choose to illustrate this through the way you speak about things. It's a form of shorthand. In day to day life it's the easiest way to ensure that people take you as you would want them to find you.

But when you want to engage an audience you need to use words and a frame of reference that will enable them to hear, digest and assimilate your message.

It's a balance. You will still have to be yourself - you are the way you speak -

but if being you comes at the expense of being unable to engage your audience then the price may be too high.

Spend some time researching your audiences.

Make what you are saying usable

Journalists do not have endless space for your message. Journalists think in terms of space - numbers of words, numbers of seconds. A journalist writing a piece for a local paper may be looking for no more than 30 words from you in quotes. A radio interview may boil down to a 36 word comment during 10 seconds of tape. This means that you have to fit your message into that space. The longer it is the more they'll have to cut - if they can. The more impenetrable it is, the less they'll want to use it. The more you make it usable text the more they'll thank you.

And, of course, the more you are able to edit what you say before you say it, the more control you will have over your message. Think about the practicalities of putting together a piece of writing or broadcasting. You will be asked a series of questions. Your comments will be written down or recorded. If they are written, journalists will read *linearly* through your comments. The stuff you say at the beginning will be read first. Key words may jump out. You need to ensure that they're the ones you'd want. If the interview is taped, the material at the beginning will be heard before the stuff at the end. Obvious. But in practical terms, when the pressure is on, a journalist may be tempted to use what they hear first rather than what might be best.

Make it active

There is a trend in public sector communication to write and communicate in the passive tense - *proposals are being brought forward* rather than *we are bringing proposals forward*. There is a tendency to miss out the *who* in communication. It may be something to do with the idea that others make decisions, we merely provide advice. But when you are talking to the media make what you are saying active.

Think about the difference that it makes. For example, *recycling collections will be stepped up* becomes *we will be stepping up recycling collections*. It not only sounds better, it feels better and it makes you sound as if you are actually taking action.

Avoid jargon

Jargon represents the kiss of death to anyone who doesn't understand the words that you are using. Jargon is a private language, a shorthand form of communication between people who know the code. It's not a problem as long as the other party speaks the same language. In fact, it's essential in much of our day to day work - if we had to unpack what *the modernisation agenda* means in health or what *CPA and best value* means in local government every five minutes we'd get little else done.

But when you are talking to journalists put your comments in plain straightforward English.

Think audience

The fact is that you can get a tick in all of the above boxes and still make what you are saying meaningful. Which is why you need to move to the next audience - the one that the journalist is communicating with. The key question you need to focus on is quite simple: *what difference will what we are saying or doing make to the lives of the people who read/see/hear this?*

III Making yourself quotable

Think top line

Don't lose sight of the fact that if what you are saying is newsworthy it will be quoted or find its way out into the world whether or not you spend much time crafting your message. Focus on what you want people to say to each other in the corridor, at the bus stop, in the pub, over dinner or at breakfast. The top line is the story - it's the *this is what we're going to do for you* line. When you are putting together your top line, don't forget the downside. For example, *we're cranking up quality now* - a line designed to say that you are radically improving the way you work, this might also say to people that *you've allowed things to slip for long enough.*

What's the sticky text?
Advertising copy writers spend a lot of time trying to come up with sticky words and phrases. This is the text that *sticks* in your mind. At its very best it's the text that becomes the new idioms. Chris Patten's *double whammy* is a brilliant example of a new phrase which has entered the language. You might be lucky enough to come up with something as good as that. You should be looking for words and phrases which stay with your audience.

It's unlikely that words from the current management lexicon are going to stick. So quickly abandon *employee-centred customer-focused empowering enabling third way solutions that enable the sensitive side of our organisation to connect with real and everyday experiences of our citizens, customers and clients in a holistic joined up third way kind of way.*

You don't need to do this every other week so you can afford to spend some time working on your quotes. Here are some places you might look for ideas:

Buy a book of idioms
Idioms, accepted phrases and ways of putting things, have the advantage that people will most probably have heard a particular form of words before. But simply repeating someone else's words won't necessarily help you unless you are able to make the words say something else. This can be done quite easily by changing the emphasis, the focus or a couple of words in the phrase. For example, you might want to make a case against GM crops and find yourself saying *better the devil we know than the devil they sow.*

Buy the tabloids
Newspapers like the *Sun* and the *Mail* are brilliant at finding ways of saying a lot in a few words. Try to read the papers in new ways and look for good

ways of putting things. Use their headlines to teach you to be brief, punchy and interesting.

Look at book titles

These work in the same way as film titles. Book and film titles (which you will find in *Halliwell's* film guide) as well as being interesting, also act as currency. We can use a title to stand in for a bigger meaning - *this issue will be his High Noon; Bordershire PCT will have to try harder or people will die harder.* You can use song titles in similar ways.

In all of these instances think about not only the meaning that will be conveyed by also what your choice of title says about you. While you could easily convey great sadness or frustration through the use of a pop song title - *this is a tragedy and we realise now that we were just like virgins in our approach* - it needs to be appropriate. Apply common sense here and you won't go far wrong.

IV Making your words speak

Getting the right words and phrases will help you to get your message across. But you'll still have to make your words speak. The tragedy is that many of us fall into the habit of sounding as though we speak in written paragraphs. Look at the following two paragraphs.

The organisation is facing a number of important challenges which we are confident it will appraise and surmount with confidence. Staff are our greatest resource. We anticipate that we will be able to engage them in the challenges ahead.

Things are going to be tough for us. But our staff are committed. They're up for those challenges and I think you'll see success in their faces and in our services.

The second should feel as though you are speaking to people. If you really want to sound real, listen to real people. When you talk through the media, you are going straight into people's lounges and into their cars. It's intimate. You've got to make it feel that way. Here's how.

Get the rhythm right

Every day speech has a rhythm. Try to capture that in the way that you speak to the media. A quick way to do this is to spend a day listening to other people. Focus on the feel of their language. You'll quickly notice that people don't speak in proper sentences. They go on and off the point. There are interjections, ums and errs. Now you won't want to put those into your press releases or interviews. But you will want them to convey that same sense of spontaneity.

Keep thinking about full stops and commas. By thinking about where they would go in your own spoken sentences you will start to develop pace and pause.

Look at these - same words (more or less), different feel.

I think we've done all we can in the last 18 months because it has been hard you know - we've worked hard, nobody would say otherwise - and I think you can see the benefits.

I think we've done all we can. The last 18 months have been tough. We've worked hard. Ask anybody. But I think you can see the benefits.

Think feelings

Before you choose your words, think about how you want your audience to feel. Think about the full gamut of emotions - from reassurance, to warm glow, to concern, to anger, to guilt. There are very few words that will cause no feelings at all - even if it's just boredom. So put the feelings on the agenda.

Three part lists

If you can turn what you're going to say into a three part list then you are more likely to get people to remember it. Remember Tony Blair's education sound-bite, *education, education, education*. Try and find three words or phrases that fit well together, especially if you want your audience to remember what you have said.

This is what it is and what it's not

This technique is often used by barristers who are acutely aware of the need to keep their audiences' attention - a jury can be apt to let its focus wander. *A contrasting pair* helps your audience locate your message in two ways. First you tell them what it's not and then you tell them what it is.

This book's not about teaching people how to manipulate the media; it's about showing them how they're manipulated by the media.

The more poignant you can make the contrast, the more effective it can be. Contrasting pairs can quickly become powerful currency since they can easily anchor your message. It's easier for our minds to hold complexity when we get a digestible explanation.

Alliteration

This is simply getting the words you use to begin with the same letter or sound. That might sound a bit vacuous but the best wordsmiths do this all the time. Again, this will help people to retain your message. Or this will make your matter memorable.

There are lots of brilliant examples but the most haunting in recent years is *Diana - the people's princess*.

Metaphor

Frequently we have to convey things of enormous complexity. Think about modernising public services. Or the choice agenda in health. Or best value in local government. Each of those terms has two distinct sets of meaning. Modernisation is something that Millie used to do when she was Julie Andrews. Choice is almost hackneyed because it's often referred to when we have none. And best value to most of us is value for money.

If we are to use terms with different meanings that we need to define to our specific audiences we can use metaphor to anchor our definition. For example, we will readily talk about the time that massive systemic change will take in the public sector. But it's a lot quicker to say that the public sector is a *supertanker*. And even though most of us have never been on one we all have a pretty good idea of what they're about - hulking, slow, masses of momentum but when they're pointing in the right direction, there's no stopping them.

Find metaphors that people can relate to. And weigh them up in terms of how they might be interpreted in the worst case scenario - *is the St. Bop supertanker now holed below the water?*

Simile

Telling people what something is like will also make it easier to get your message across. When looking for similes try to find an example that your audience can relate to - *they've managed the budget like a teenager with a new credit card from the Live Fast Die Young bank.*

V Same words, different mouths - making it all fit together

In the end, you can't divorce people from words. The same words can have different meanings and impact when spoken by different people. So think about these things when you choose the speaker.

What would add credibility?

The phrase "I know that this will be better for patients" will always be more believable when coming from a doctor. And in a radio interview, for example, the introduction - *we'll be talking to Dr. Smith in a moment about her experiences in Bradgate Acute Trust* - can render practically everything that she says meaningful and credible.

If you want some objective data on which professions people are likely to believe the most, take a look at www.mori.com.

What are their personal qualities?

John Wayne once said that if you want people to listen to you walk slow, talk slow and don't say much. Brilliant if that's you. But it may not be. People who speak quickly will convey different qualities - enthusiasm, energy, dynamism. But they can also convey panic, rush and being out of control.

When you are managing a crisis for example, you will want to select the slow talker - it will help you to convey reassurance, calm and organisation. And all you'll have to worry about is persuading your fast-talking, no-stopping chief executive that someone else should do the public statements.

Do they feel comfortable with the words?

The words have got to feel right for the speaker. When you are building sound-bites it's best to listen first to the person you expect to say them. Ideally, as well as talking in the language of the listener they ought to convey the essence of the speaker. And this will raise a difficult issue - if the speaker can't talk the listener's language.

You need to be honest. Some people simply can't tone it down. They live, eat and breathe jargon. Make sure that the speaker is able to feel comfortable with the words you expect them to use. And never forget that we are all very adept at hearing the discomfort of someone saying something that they don't really believe themselves. It will make your whole message sound like a lie.

Can they make them their own?

The more you can weld your key messages into the day to day idioms of your speaker, making it flow naturally, the more likely we are to believe what they are saying. This is more likely to happen if the person either has time to prepare or if they are an experienced presenter. If you are preparing a sound-bite, allow time to play with the text and make it feel real.

Can they add a personal touch?

Look for opportunities for the speaker to bring in their own experience. We are more likely to believe someone if we think they've seen what they're talking about first hand. That's not to say that you can't use people who have no direct experience. They can bring this into what they say by citing people who do the job - *"I know how hard doctors are finding this. I was talking to our doctors on their rounds just yesterday and they were saying..."*

Why does all this matter?

Journalists will test what you say. They will probe. They will listen for comments that sound disingenuous. We can all hear it. And they will push you, or your staff, into admitting things that they believe but feel that they can't say. Confession may be good for the soul, but on air confession can be very bad for your career and your organisation's reputation.

10 Killer facts

A single fact, well presented, can change the way we feel about an entire issue.

In earlier chapters you will have learned that the way you tell a story will make a difference to the way that people feel about it. Killer facts and killer quotes are often what turns a story one way rather than another.

The idea behind a killer fact is to find a single fact or single quote that captures the essence of a story. And that does one very important thing:

It changes the way that people feel about an issue so much that they are prepared to tell someone else about it.

A killer fact ought to have a killer reaction. In a single stroke, it will affect how your key audience feels about something.

Killer facts are like viruses - they spread from person to person very quickly.

How to write killer facts

Start with facts

Facts are often better than opinions as a way of getting a message across. After all, you may be indignant about a particular thing but unless you are very important most people are likely to say, "so what?!" Facts on the other hand should speak for themselves. With killer facts, you want people to pass them round - so the freer they are of apparent bias, the better.

It's worth spending time in your organisation sorting out the key facts. In a hospital, for example, how many operations you carry out every year, or the number of extra years of life you have created for your patients as a result of those operations. In a school, you could talk about the destinations of pupils who used to be at the school (10% of the country's top company directors are former pupils). Councils can talk not only about the range of their services but their nature.

Know your audience

Like any communication, it's best to shape not only what you say but how you say it for the audience you are speaking to. For example, you may be trying to convey killer facts about smoking. But whereas references to the number of millilitres of tar produced in the UK every day could quickly become technical - *the average consumption of tar is 0.17 ml per capita* - this would quickly come to life when you say that the average smoker consumes the equivalent of a gallon of tar in his or her lifetime.

So be clear about who your audience is, what their experiences are, how they make sense of the world. You can make certain assumptions here. People with children will tend to see the world in terms of their family, the things that are likely affect their health and wellbeing and the stability of their home. People who are career-minded might think about the chances of progression, office-politics, money, how to get to the top.

Decide what kind of reaction you are looking for

The same fact put in different ways will elicit different reactions. There are lots of ways of looking at the same fact. Essentially, you are asking yourself - and you may want to test this with other people - *how would I want to put this fact in order that this audience would feel sad or angry or guilty.*

Don't expect this to be easy. It will take time first to *frame* the facts and then to establish whether your facts make people feel the way that you think they should.

Make them simple

The object of using facts in your arguments is to get your message across as quickly and effectively as possible. And two things are clear - the more obscure the language you use the harder it will be for the reader or listener - and that goes for jargon; the more complex the sentence structure you use the less likely you will be to engage your reader.

For example:

Untoward incidences arising from the excessive consumption of substances which alter states of consciousness accounted for 23 deaths in the last seven working days.

Drinking killed 23 people in the last two weeks.

Make them currency and think about how other people will use them

Ideally, you want to send out your killer facts and make them so strong that other people will want to pass them on for you. Killer facts can be the sort of stuff that people say to each other in the car park, at the photocopier, in the pub or, dare I say it, at the water cooler.

This is a real challenge. But it's worth taking the time to think about what's going to get people talking. Mostly, people will talk about things that affect them and theirs directly. Killer facts:

▲ Can change behaviour

▲ Can give them ammunition to change other people's behaviour

▲ Can give them *bullets to fire* - facts and figures

▲ Can give them something to say to people when they're stuck for something to say

▲ Can give them *you'll never guesses*

Think about it this way: if you appear on the radio today and release one of your killer facts you want it to be the kind of fact that listeners will so want to hang onto that they will say it over and over to themselves before they tell someone else.

One of the implications is that you begin writing your killer facts *with other people's arguments in your head.*

Your facts become solutions to their problems.

Smoking in pubs. I hate it. And I know I'm not alone. So if I wanted to create a body of opinion against smoking in pubs I'd want to give others who feel the same as me ammunition they could use to make life uncomfortable for smokers.

These are made up. But imagine:

A non-smoker who goes out for a drink on a Friday night will have smoked the equivalent of 10,000 cigarettes by the time he is 35.

A non-smoker going to a pub on a Saturday night will have so much smoke in their clothes that the smell can be detected in the street ten metres away.

The total amount of smoke in British pubs during the average weekend is the equivalent of a five day smog covering London.

Try them out
The quickest way to do this - although it isn't exactly scientific - is to tell someone one of your killer facts in passing and see when it comes back.

Putting killer facts to work
Write them - go through the process and identify 10, say, killer facts for each of the areas you want to promote this year. Take the time it will need.

Learn and share them - make sure that you know them and that everyone else who needs to know them does. Think about how you might share them inside the organisation. Look at other media - it's relatively cheap to publish postcards, for example, and these can be a powerful way of getting your facts around the organisation.

Use them as often as possible - if you're really going to make them work for you, it's best to use every and all available means, tempered, of course, by the realisation that the same facts won't necessarily work for every audience.

Killer facts - an example

Persuading people that smoking is dangerous

Smoking kills over 120,000 people in the UK every year - or more than 13 people every hour. Most die from three main diseases associated with smoking: cancer, chronic obstructive lung disease (bronchitis or emphysema) and coronary heart disease;

Passive smoking is estimated to kill several hundred people a year. It can cause pneumonia, asthma, cot death and possibly neurobiological impairment in children. Around 17,000 children under the age of five are admitted to hospital every year with illnesses resulting from passive smoking;

The cost to the NHS of treating smoking-related illnesses is around £1.7bn a year. Because an estimated one in three cigarettes smoked in the UK are smuggled, the country loses a further £3.8bn in lost tax revenues;

Smoking in pregnancy can cause low birth weights. Those babies are also statistically more likely to suffer illness or death during their first year of life.

Source: www.guardian.co.uk

11 Living on air

If you are able to present your message well through the broadcast media you will add weight to what you have to say. MORI research shows that television news is probably the most trusted in the UK. But broadcasting presents its own challenges. You need to think about how you look and how you sound as well as what you say.

Focus on your key message early

Broadcasters tend to squeeze their news into tighter packages than newspapers. Complex ideas are simplified and turned into pieces lasting seconds. What you say will be hacked about and processed. So be prepared for what you want to say. And what you don't. Start by assuming that journalists will want to boil your remarks down to a single comment. Make that your key message and get it into the interview as early as possible.

Be ready for the experience

You can reasonably expect to find out who the interview is with, if someone with an opposing view will also be there, and whether it will be live or chopped about and mixed with other people's views. Technology has made it possible for remote studios to be sited anywhere. You might never meet your interviewer face to face. It'll feel like talking into space with no cues from your interviewer (it spoils the play back).

Do as much thinking and preparation as you can beforehand, but avoid referring to notes. On TV it looks like you are not sure what you're talking about, and on radio it sounds like it. Remember, you are there to entertain as well as inform. If you are dull, or insist on explaining minute detail, you will quickly be dispatched.

Going live

This can give you more space and
more control, as what you say
goes out unedited. Make your
point in the first answer as there
might not be another chance.
Everything else should support
that initial point. Watch out for
silences during the interview.
Journalists and presenters can use
eye contact or nod agreeably to
encourage you to fill them up. You could
leave yourself exposed by saying things you hadn't planned to.

Recorded interviews

Journalists will be hunting for soundbites of no more than 20 seconds. And
they'll ask lots of different questions until they get them. Make sure you stick
to your line. Re-word your answer so that it fits each question. At best your
contribution might be two or three of those soundbites.

On site

Journalists who come to you are looking for sights and sounds as well as your
words. They'll want everything placed at their disposal to get the job done
swiftly. They may move the interview spot to a location where your words have
a backdrop. Think - if you're saying that your organisation does not pollute and
there's a belching chimney behind you (even if it's not yours) do you think you
will be believed?

Studio discussion

Get your view in at the earliest part of the discussion. Your chances reduce as
the programme moves on. Don't get too distracted by the specifics of the

question. Mould the answer you want to give so it looks like it's a natural response, using a couple of words from the question.

It's a different kind of relationship

When you are interviewed by a print journalist, the questions that you are asked will not (except in some magazine formats) appear in print. Only your direct quotes and paraphrased comments will be there. The interview will be framed by the journalist. Your comments will only really make sense in the context of the whole piece. The same can happen in recorded broadcasts. In so-called packages, your voice can appear in voice-over and in comment without the question that you were asked being broadcast. There is no opportunity for you to re-frame your comments.

However, in a studio discussion and in a live interview you can create a new relationship - one with the listener or viewer. You can talk to them directly by allowing them to be the judge of reasonableness in the questions you are asked. Put yourself in the audience's place when you are being interviewed. Think about how you will sound and look to them.

Texture - the tone of voice and the look

One of the key ways in which we make judgements about people is whether they present a *consonant* image. We expect there to be a fit between what they are saying and how they look or sound. If you are to present yourself consonantly then you need to be honest about how you come across. This means looking at your salient personal qualities. Better still, get someone to give you an honest appraisal.

If your message is caring and warm, your voice needs to be saying the same. If you are presenting a humanistic, *we care about people* message, then you need to look warm and friendly. If your natural facial expression is a scowl the audience is unlikely to be convinced. If you look away, or if your eyes dot from side to side, then what you will be saying visually may clash with your central message.

Consider the aftermath

Get someone to tape your contribution so that you can review it and learn. If your comments have been genuinely misunderstood or taken out of context ring the journalist and tell them. But don't phone if you simply don't like the angle they've taken - you'll be wasting your time.

Create opportunities

Keep on top of current affairs and offer yourself as a commentator on news topics if you have something to add. Local TV and radio especially are always hungry for a local angle, and even national programmes with daily schedules to fill will listen to a likely contributor.

And finally...

Broadcasters are always looking for "light and shade". They know that too much hard news depresses the listener. There will always be a space for the funny story that's not all that new, just untold, for the fascinating and for the "feature". Non-news radio is just as hungry for material. Invite programmes to come and do a feature, or even a full show, on your sector.

12 Risk and media relations

Here are some tips to think about when considering how to manage media opportunities.

Define success

Try to find a way of measuring the benefits of media opportunities in your organisation. Identify units in which you can evaluate each.

Weigh up the opportunity

What's in it for your organisation? There are all sorts of ways to look at benefits.

▲ It may give you an opportunity to get a key message across to an important audience

▲ It may be better that you do the interview than a colleague who may be less skilled

▲ It may help you to build a relationship with a journalist

▲ It may be the least damaging option - the journalist may be writing the story anyway

Weigh up the risks

There may be bear traps - issues could be brought up that you haven't thought about or you don't want to have to deal with. This can be worse in a live broadcast interview.

▲ You may be unable to manage the line of questioning

▲   You may give away news that you hadn't planned to share

▲ You may be unable to manage the interview stress

▲ You may not be the right person - there may be someone who would have an interest in this either organisationally, politically or managerially

Look at the potential disbenefits

▲ You may look evasive if you don't do the interview

▲ Someone else beyond your control or influence may do it anyway

▲ The story could run without you

▲ You might be cited as a "no comment" or "refused to be interviewed"

Take a good look at it and then reach a view.

Don't automatically assume that just because you get a call from a journalist that you should do the interview. As the saying goes, sometimes it's better to say nothing and be thought a fool than to speak and put the matter beyond any doubt.

Look at the audience - do you need to talk to them?

Be clear about who you would be talking to. Most of the interviews you are likely to do will be with the local newspaper or radio station. Get some information on who listens and when or what kind of readership the paper has. Create a visual picture of who you would be talking to, what their concerns are and, if it's radio or television, what they would be doing when they are taking in your message.

Do you have a clear message?

Decide what you are saying about this issue or subject. Write it down in advance and share it with colleagues. It should fit in with your departmental goals or plans. There's no point in saying one thing and doing another - easily done if your message is about aspirations or, worse, your own views. It won't take long for a journalist to track down someone who will be prepared to point out the contradiction.

Is it written down?

Don't make this up as you go along. You should have some key messages for each issue you are trying to manage. At the same time, you will want to have departmental or organisational key messages - those that relate to what you are trying to achieve.

Do you have killer facts?

Have a list of killer facts that can be dropped into your responses that demonstrate your message. It will do no harm to have them by the phone if it's a telephone interview. Better still, learn them so that you can easily use them. Make sure that they're written in a form that sounds conversational. It will be easier to slip into them if they feel spoken. If you have to use a link that sounds like - *I wonder if in order to illustrate this point I might quote from some statistics* - then you may not sound so convincing.

Are you prepared?

You may be the most amazing multi-skilled person in the world, but you shouldn't underestimate the potential impact of a tough interview. It may be, of course, that you are about to be interviewed on a subject you know well by a journalist you've been working with for ages. In which case, fine.

But if this is a relatively new experience for you, if you are unclear about the message you will need longer to prepare. You may want to rehearse a possible interview with someone from your communications department.

Have you thought of the questions you could be asked?

Start with the questions that relate to the matter in hand. Look at the different ways into the subject. Imagine, for example, that you are about to close a community centre. A journalist could look at this from any number of angles:

▲ Impact - isn't it fair to say that this closure will devastate the lives of local people?

▲ Process - would you not agree that you have completely ignored the need to consult local people?

▲ Motive - this isn't about making better use of resources it's about settling old scores, that's the case, isn't it?

▲ Personal - clearly the council believes that it has to take this decision, but it must be one that you are personally uncomfortable with?

▲ Hidden agendas - let's be honest, you're starting a consultation on this community centre today but you've already made up your minds and it's closing, that's the reality, isn't it?

▲ Contradictions - the truth is this, you are quite willing to close community centres to save money but you are still paying hundreds of thousands of pounds in members' allowances, that's a bit rich isn't it?

▲ Internal disquiet - you say that everyone is behind this closure but the fact is that several leading members of the executive are refusing to endorse it, that's true isn't it? Or: we've been talking to your staff and the reality is rather more simple than you present it - your staff say you haven't made your case, you haven't got a case for closure and you're simply following the wishes of your political masters blindly, that's true isn't it?

Have you thought of other questions that could be around?

Public organisations never manage one issue at a time. At any given moment there will be many decisions in the managerial and political pipeline. And you will need to consider whether the interview that you are being invited to take part in isn't just a ruse to get you to answer questions that you might otherwise want to avoid.

Journalists may use this approach to lure you into the area. And it can be hard to resist. If your interview is with a print journalist you can simply refuse to be drawn. But if you're in the middle of a live broadcast interview, the questions can be put to you in such a way as to make you sound totally unreasonable if you refuse to comment.

Does the time suit you?

The timing of a message can be as important as the message itself. Think about how the interview fits in with your existing plans to get your message out. Look at the best time in terms of reaching the audience you want to reach - your local BBC station may want to get you in for an afternoon show chat whilst you might want to reach a drive time audience. Look at the other pressures on your time - don't disadvantage yourself by having to rush through the interview.

Can you exert control?

You will not be able to control the questions. But you can control the answers. If you feel that you are likely to get led into blind alleys take a look at chapter 15 (eyeball to eyeball). Bear in mind that *if you don't say it, they can't use it.* You can control or significantly influence the location of the interview although journalists may seek to influence you with comments about better lighting for the camera, better ambience for the radio and so on.

You can also control how you look. Clearly you won't be able to drastically alter your appearance the same day an interview is booked. But think about the audience you are talking to and about the message you are likely to give out with an unaltered appearance. Various research reports have shown that 70 - 80% of the message that others read is visual. You will be saying more with your appearance than you will with your mouth. Think about that.

Be clear also about what you will not talk about. The more *important* you are the more you are likely to be called upon to comment on wider issues. You need to determine whether you are going to make comments. Don't be suckered into giving personal views.

What's the worst case scenario

Try to weigh up the worst that could happen as a result of the media opportunity. Decide whether you can live with that. Use this to inform your decision-making process.

Did it work?

Afterwards, weigh it up. Look at the combination of what you said and how you appeared (if it was television, or how you sounded if it was radio) with what you were trying to achieve with the interview. Did it deliver? It's best to ask for honest feedback. The problem that public figures have is that they can quickly become shorthand for the organisation itself. A senior manager who stumbles his or her way through an interview sounding incoherent and boring says that about their organisation.

The clearer you are about what a successful outcome would be the better you will be able to evaluate risk.

13 Managing the media in a crisis

There's a temptation in a crisis to forget every rule in the book - such can be the pressure, the pace and the panic around you. But if you are the chosen communicator, the one person who needs to keep a bit of detachment and an eye on the big picture is you.

What is a crisis?

It's best to treat anything that will significantly affect confidence in your organisation or key individuals as a crisis. That could be anything from a physical disaster to a fraud.

Spend some time taking stock. Look at the issues that could affect how people see you. Identify the news hot-spots. In health, it could be how you plan for the winter. It will be when you are inspected by the likes of the Commission for Health Improvement. And then there are serious untoward incidents.

A good deal of potential crises can be forecast and prepared for. Don't ignore, however, other less predictable potential crises. An organisation that is closely associated with an individual can be adversely affected if that person is involved in a controversy.

Be ready for it

Take time out way before it happens to think about some scenarios that fit the descriptions above. Being ready doesn't just mean writing down possibilities. It means starting to think about the resource implications and the logistics. It's very easy to underestimate the impact that even a minor crisis can have.

For example, imagine your organisation gets a particularly damning inspection report from one of the main public sector inspectorates. First, the media will probably be briefed about it pretty soon after you will. Second, they may have an agenda and could (and this is where you will need to understand the key people in your relevant media) make a big issue out of it. That will require you to prepare your position and deliver it in an interview, a statement or some form of public event. Third, that may precipitate a further reaction. It may be that there is little news at the time, thereby giving you more (unwanted) space. Or others may wade into the row. Or other media may be attracted.

And meanwhile, the hours rack up - agreeing statements, rehearsing Q&As, not doing your day job, anticipating the next interview.

Write down and prepare for possible scenarios

What is the disaster top ten at your council? What are the worst things that could happen to your Trust? Write them down, prepare the positions you might take, identify who would deliver them, develop protocols to ensure that only the right people talk to the media during this time and try them out for size. Don't wait until the worst happens before you deal with it. That would be a disaster.

Link this into your emergency planning arrangements.

Have physical contingency plans

Press calls can come in hundreds; you could be knee deep in TV crews. Who will help, will your phone system cope, where will you put people? Who will organise it? Waiting until they arrive is too late.

Think about who would take charge in those circumstances. Prepare staff who might be affected - for example, reception staff will need to know that journalists are not allowed on site without your permission. Identify a space where journalists could be put - it could be prepared with fax machines, access to the Internet, spaces to film, telephone lines.

Managing the media in a crisis

Don't underestimate the impact of a media frenzy. A good (or bad) news story can quickly mean journalists appearing on your patch. When Nigel Mansell was taken to a Nottingham hospital after a motor racing accident the media knew about it before the hospital press office.

- ▲ You will need to have people who can handle phone calls

- ▲ You will need to have a means by which statements can be drafted and agreed

- ▲ You should have top staff ready and prepared to talk to the media

- ▲ The telephone numbers of key people should be available to the press office or communications team

- ▲ You will need people who are skilled in interviews

- ▲ You will need to be coordinated and in control

Don't underestimate the ingenuity of a journalist

If a story is important enough, journalists will go to all sorts of lengths to get it. That might mean going through official channels. But it might equally mean, getting the story no matter what. Stories of journalists dressing up as doctors to get access to patients are not uncommon. They may call and pretend to be a patient's relative.

When a crisis happens...

Say sorry
You don't have to take responsibility for the event. But you can still express your sympathy. Think about what people would expect you to say and say as much of that as you reasonably can.

Keep talking
What the media want is information, information and information. And if

they're not getting it from you they will go somewhere else and you've lost your role as messenger. Even if information is sketchy keep giving updates when you can. If you promise regular briefings make sure you deliver.

Keep control by being flexible
If the story is big enough you'll get a media camp on your doorstep. Why not give them a facility that keeps them warm and better-tempered, and out of sight? Build relationships where you can. They have a job to do and they will do it no matter what. Work with them to try to get the best for both sides.

Be honest
If you lie it will at some stage come out. If you don't want to make a particular fact public, don't. But where certain truths are inevitable, say them. If they're dragged out of you, or exposed after the event, it could damage your organisation.

Keep in contact
Stay in touch with the managers of the crisis, with what the media are saying about the crisis, and with others issuing information about the crisis (such as Police or Fire PR).

Stay on top
Keep on top of the main questions in the story: What has happened? A summary of the crisis from your organisation's perspective - but be prepared to redirect the questions someone else should be answering. On a breaking news story the media will take information from anyone. In a fire they'll ask you about how it was tackled and the fire service about what your organisation had inside the building - and they'll use the answers that anyone gives them.

What is your organisation doing about it? Right now, later, tomorrow and next week. Who is being put up to talk? If you are doing all of the above, you could be too busy and fraught to look and sound calm. Give the job to someone who is good at it and close to the crisis. If the crisis lasts for any period of time, be prepared to put up fresh faces to satisfy the media's immense desire for the re-versioning of stories.

Don't forget that how you manage a crisis can determine how key audiences might feel about your organisation. So think about how you look as well as what you do.

14 Fighting back

You won't always get the press you think you deserve. Managers frequently complain of being misquoted or misrepresented.

Check the reasonableness of your case

You may not like the coverage you get on a particular story but that's not to say that it's unreasonable. Challenging journalists on stories can get heated very quickly. In all probability, if the story is contentious, staff at the publication or in the programme will have thought at least twice about it before publishing. A challenge will get to the heart of their personal credibility - accuracy is critical for the media - and they are likely to defend their ground.

Be clear about your facts before you take any actions. And when you challenge, make the basis of your challenge clear.

Make a judgement about the outcome of a challenge

This is one step beyond the reasonableness check. In essence, this means asking yourself whether a challenge will make things better or worse. For example, you may question a story and win the right of reply. In the next edition, or next bulletin, your side of the story or your response to the original report is run. What then? Will it clear the matter up? Or will it precipitate further coverage. Think about whether it is wise - in terms of the net impression that your key audiences might have - to let the thing lie.

Be constructive

Challenging the media in the first instance is a matter of negotiation. There is little to be gained from bullying. You will still have to work with them after this story has been and gone. Whatever happens you want to have a relationship which will benefit your organisation in the end.

Set out your case, clearly and cogently. Make clear where you believe the story misrepresented you.

Don't cut off your nose

One approach to negative media coverage is to threaten withdrawal of cooperation. This might take the form of not sending press releases to the media, not allowing interviews with key people, favouring the competition. It may make you feel a lot better. But it's unlikely to work for you in the long run. Most of your news - public reports - will be news anyway. You're obliged to make them available. Journalists will always be able to find someone in your organisation to talk to. And in the mean time bad blood could breed bad coverage.

Neither is it very wise to threaten to withdraw advertising, print contracts or distribution work.

Make a rapid response

If you do have a problem with a report, then you must act quickly. First, because the earlier you react the more promptly a correction can be published. Second, because your reaction time will be read as an indicator of the seriousness with which you are making a challenge. If you wait three weeks to complain about a story you are unlikely to be taken seriously at all.

If you are worried about coverage you should monitor reports and be in a position to respond quickly. Some councils monitor radio broadcasts live. You may not need to go that far if errant items are few and far between. But you should look at newspapers.

Speak to the journalist concerned and make your points succinctly. It is likely that anyone you speak to during the day will be busy. Be clear about what you want in return. Refer to the Press Complaints Commission's code of practice. This is a voluntary code but it talks about giving *due prominence* to corrections.

You may find that the journalist is either unwilling or unable to give you satisfaction. You should then follow this up immediately with a call to either the news editor or the editor. Follow the same process making your objections clear.

If relationships break down

Relationships between public sector organisations and the media can break down. In the heat of the moment, or under pressure from others, things can be said which might be better left unsaid. If this happens, create the earliest possible opportunity to meet with the journalists and the editor to re-establish relationships. The reality is that you need them and they need you. Believing the reverse is unlikely to result in better coverage. And like it or not, people do believe what they read, see and hear in the media.

If you're still not happy

You can make a complaint to the Press Complaints Commission. Its code of practice is printed at the end of this book.

Its contact details are:
Press Complaints Commission, 1 Salisbury Square, London EC4Y 8JB
Help Line: 020 7353 3732
Switchboard: 020 7353 1248 E-mail: complaints@pcc.org.uk

If you are unhappy with a broadcast, you can complain to the Broadcasting Standards Commission.

Its contact details are:
Broadcasting Standards Commission, 7 The Sanctuary, London SW1P 3JS
Telephone: 020 7808 1000 Fax: 020 7233 0397 e-mail: bsc@bsc.org.uk

15 Eyeball to eyeball - interviews

This chapter will look at three areas

    I   Interviews in general

    II   The anatomy of an interview

    III   Questioning techniques

I Interviews in general

Interviews are one of the key aspects of any relationship with the media. Whereas journalists may report what they hear at public meetings, or reproduce what you send in as press releases, the interview is an opportunity to bring the issue to life. It's the *you heard it from the horse's mouth* part of journalism.

Our thinking about interviews has probably been skewed in recent years by the way in which high profile combative exchanges have become part of our daily lives. Radio Four's *Today* programme is forever in the news itself because someone or other has criticised it for putting too much pressure on a particular interviewee. Or it gets criticised for continually interrupting interviewees and not allowing them to speak.

We will look at difficult interviews later in this chapter but for the moment, though, let's look at what the interview is there for.

They are about information and understanding

Interviews are intended to find out what you have to say about an issue or event. The journalist will want to know and be able to record what you are saying and what you are not prepared to say on a particular subject. If he or she is rigorous they will test each of your remarks in order to clarify both what you are saying and what it might mean.

They are about clarity

In day to day life, much of what we say is vague. The whole of the public sector is soaked through with expressions which don't really mean much at all. If you want to find examples of this, look to your organisation's mission statement. It is not hard to find statements in education about *meeting the needs of the whole child*. In local government, people will regularly talk about *capacity building and empowerment*. In health, people will talk about *modernisation and choice*. But what these mean in reality will often not stand closer scrutiny.

They focus on who said what to whom when and why or who did what to whom and with what effect?

Interviews are about specifics. In that sense they have a great deal in common with exchanges in court. A journalist will feel quite at liberty to pursue an interviewee to establish what they are and what they are not saying. What's more, they will want to know what something *means*. It is very easy for public service managers to slip into jargon and to hide behind well worn phrases. Journalists will unpack your words by seeking to explain what they mean or might mean to ordinary people.

The agenda is different for the media than it may be for you

In reality, vague and obtuse phrases can have a meaning - they are embedded in organisational and operational practice. They can be very useful since they can help to move things on. In an organisation which is trying to build relationships with the private sector a simple commitment from the leader of the council or the chairman that they are keen to *work in partnership* will go a long way.

But in the real world - that occupied by journalists and their readers, listeners and viewers - this currency doesn't always cut much ice. And using what amounts to no more than jargon will force the journalist to force you to be more specific.

Take the idea that you may want to say to a number of key audiences that you are *working in partnership* with another public sector provider. Partnership is one of the most overused words of the first part of this century. If you are being interviewed about partnership the journalist could well want to know the answers to a lot of questions you might not even have considered.

- ▲ What will you do in partnership?
- ▲ What difference will it make?
- ▲ What will you actually do?
- ▲ Who will pay for it all?
- ▲ Who is really in charge of this thing?
- ▲ What happens if it all goes wrong?
- ▲ What plans have you put in place to ensure it doesn't?

In other words, the journalists will want to know what it all means in terms of the *people who watch, read or listen to this media report*. The difficulty you may face, and this is most stark in a live interview, is not knowing the answers to questions which listeners or viewers would want to ask.

II The anatomy of an interview

Before the interview

Before you go into an interview you should be clear about why the journalist wants to interview you. There will be two questions you will need an answer to. First, what did they say they wanted to talk to you about? Second, what might they really want to talk about? The first is pretty straightforward. And you should be told this when they call. The second is more complex since you will need to be aware of the kinds of things that could be rumbling around in your organisation at this time.

Next, you should be clear about what you want out of the interview. You should, ideally, have a key message you want to get across. Clearly, there will be a number of questions to deal with related to the subject under discussion. But the way that you deal with these ought to be organised before the interview starts.

You should also be clear about who you will be talking to. Again, there are two elements. First, who is the journalist? What do you know about them? What are their interests? What experience do you have of dealing with this person? Do you have a relationship with them already?

Second, which audience are they writing for or broadcasting to? The way you shape your key message will be a product of the audience you are seeking to address. There is more on this under key messages.

Managing the scope of the interview

It is not unreasonable for you to agree what the scope of the interview should be. But if the journalist is particularly interested in a certain subject, particularly if the interview is live, then they will want to pursue the issue anyway. You will then need to think about how you will handle what is no less than evasion.

There are other ways in which you can manage the direction of the interview. You can fill the space by keeping on talking. You can set the direction of the interview early and stick to it. You can keep returning to your central point. And you can determine how long you will be interviewed for as well as where and when it will take place.

Control of the interview

The convention which determines the interview is quite straightforward. The journalist will attempt to control the direction of the interview through the way in which he or she asks questions. Experienced managers will be able to assert control in the way they steer their remarks.

III Questioning techniques

Open questions

Open questions - those to which there is no definite right or wrong answer - are very useful in a number of ways. First, they get the interview going. Second, they can give a journalist the chance to hear how the interviewee answers questions - the style, the speed, the references they make, the techniques they use to talk round subjects. Third, they can allow the interviewee to get all of the points out that they want to make and effectively create a platform on which the interview can take place.

These questions are innocuous enough. But the danger for the interviewee is knowing when to stop. It may be that your message is pretty clear in which case an open question can give you the chance to say it uninterrupted. But if you are encouraged to speak by a journalist who simply looks at you enquiringly and nods, then you may be tempted to keep going. The longer you do so, the more likely it will be that you will stray into territory that you haven't fully thought through. If you are starting to think that you may be rambling, stop. Better still, stop before you start.

How to handle open questions:

▲ Know what you are going to say and say it

▲ Don't allow your fertile imagination to take you into the land of possibilities unless you've been there first when you were awake

▲ Be aware of the doors that you are opening up with apparently safe general comments and only open those where you know what's behind them

Closed questions

These are yes or no questions. A pointed closed question can be a dangerous thing and if you don't want to answer it, don't. The key thing about closed questions - *is this or is this not a waste of public money* - is anticipation. When you are at the weighing up stage before you do the interview, you should be thinking about how you will handle pointed questions. The rules of engagement are slightly different for different media. In a press interview an adept interviewee can talk and walk round pointed questions. In a live radio or television interview a determined journalist can simply ask the same pointed closed question over and over again.

Look again at Michael Howard's now famous interview with Jeremy Paxman about the dismissal of Derek Lewis, Head of the Prison Service. It took place on Newsnight on the 13th of May 1997.

Paxman: *Did you threaten to overrule him?*

Howard: *I was not entitled to instruct Derek Lewis and I did not instruct him...*

Paxman: *Did you threaten to overrule him?*

Howard: *The truth of the matter is that Mr. Marriot was not suspended-*

Paxman: *Did you threaten to overrule him?*

Howard: *I did not overrule Derek Lewis-*

Paxman: *Did you threaten to overrule him?*

Howard: *I took advice on what I could or could not do-*

Paxman: *Did you threaten to overrule him?*

Howard: *and acted scrupulously in accordance with that advice. I did not overrule Derek Lewis-*

Paxman: *Did you threaten to overrule him?*

Howard: *Mr. Marriot would not suspend him-*

Paxman: *Did you threaten to overrule him?*

Howard: *I have accounted for my decision to dismiss Derek Lewis-*

Paxman: *Did you threaten to overrule him?*

Howard: *-in great detail before the House of Commons-*

Paxman: *I note that you're not answering the question whether you threatened to overrule him.*

Howard: *Well, the important aspect of this which it's very clear to bear in mind-*

Paxman: *I'm sorry, I'm going to be frightfully rude but - I'm sorry - it's a straight yes-or-no question and a straight yes-or-no answer: did you threaten to overrule him?*

Howard: *I discussed the matter with Derek Lewis. I gave him the benefit of my opinion. I gave him the benefit of my opinion in strong language, but I did not instruct him because I was not, er, entitled to instruct him. I was entitled to express my opinion and that is what I did.*

Paxman: *With respect, that is not answering the question of whether you threatened to overrule him.*

Howard: *It's dealing with the relevant point which was what I was entitled to do and what I was not entitled to do, and I have dealt with this in detail before the House of Commons and before the select committee.*

Paxman: *But with respect you haven't answered the question of whether you threatened to overrule him.*

Howard: *Well, you see, the question is...*

(Source: www.bbc.co.uk)

It is highly unlikely that you will meet the likes of Jeremy Paxman in your dealings with journalists but the point remains: you will be asked closed questions and in a live interview you will need to think about how listeners or viewers are likely to feel about any techniques you employ to avoid answering them.

Funnels

This is where questions begin more generally and then home in on specifics. If an interview starts with a wide open question allowing you to say your piece, the journalist can move from those initial comments into matters of great detail. The challenge for you is to ensure that the territory that is then explored is land on which you feel comfortable.

For example:

Q: *Tell me about your approach to helping disaffected children to learn.*

A: *We believe in meeting the needs of all of our children whether or not they are disaffected. It's worth registering that one in three children is disaffected at some point in their school career.*

Q: *It's fair to say, though, is it not, that as children get towards the end of their school career, before say the age of 16, that this group of disaffected children hardens, as it were?*

A: *It's certainly true that once children have disengaged it can be harder to engage them as they get closer to the point where they might want to leave us - but my point remains, one in three children will become disaffected at some point in their school career.*

Q: *Fine. But let's be honest, as disaffected children get closer to the point where they are about to leave you it can be harder to motivate staff to try to change their minds - in other words, it's better to focus on your successes rather than your failures?*

A: *We work with all children - one in three children at some point in their school career...*

Q: *Are you telling me that you don't know the group of people who are disaffected - those who are about to leave?*

A: *We know our pupils well...*

Q: *The truth is this is it not - that there is a group of children in your school which you have quite frankly given up on?*

And so on. The journalist will pursue this question until they get close to the answer they think exists - which may be based on another interview with parents or disaffected teachers - that the school is letting fifteen year olds run riot because they can neither control them, interest them nor get staff to teach them.

The journalist has managed to turn a story which the school might have seen as *all children get disaffected sometimes* into *school abandons trouble-makers*.

Reverse funnels

The same thing can work in reverse. A journalist can begin the interview ostensibly talking about an issue that you may wish to talk about. In a reverse funnel they will want to turn the specifics into the general. This technique can be used to turn innocuous safe stories into reputation-threatening issues.

For example: here's an interview about a public body investing money in Gaelic as a minority language. Good news, you might think.

Q: *Tell me about this investment that you have made - I believe that you, as an education department, have invested millions of pounds in the teaching of Gaelic as a minority language.*

A: *Yes, that's right. We believe that Gaelic, which is a key part of our culture, should be supported. It's a language that means a great deal to Scotland which is why we have invested £5.2 million in helping to develop it.*

Q: *You believe it's a good use of public money to support minority languages, to solidify their place in Scottish culture?*

A: *Yes, absolutely. We must not ignore languages just because they are spoken by a minority of the population.*

Q: *Do you support all minority languages in this way?*

A: *I'm not sure I follow...*

Q: *Well, what about Urdu, Gujerati, Hindi - how much money are you investing in supporting them?*

A: *Well, that's not really a matter for us - that would be something that the likes of social services would be interested in...I could find out for you.*

Q: *Does that not seem racist to you?*

A: *I'm sorry?*

Q: *Well, you said a moment ago that you believed it was important to support minority languages to solidify their place in Scottish culture and yet it only applies to Gaelic - other minority languages, non-indigenous languages, don't get educational support.*

A: (Yawning gap).

This interview starts with a very specific good news item and ends up making the interviewee look awkward. In a press interview it could turn out as a story highlighting the different levels of investment (none versus £5.2 million) in different minority languages. That coupled with adverse comment from community groups saying that it's unfair and institutionally racist could spawn a *public body lambasted over racist language funding* story. In a broadcast interview, the interviewee could look very uncomfortable indeed.

How to deal with funnels:

▲ Be clear about your message

▲ Think about where the line of questioning could go and anticipate it

▲ Be aware of where it is going and keep coming back to your central message

▲ Don't allow yourself to be forced to deal with questions that you hadn't anticipated unless you are very sure of your ground

▲ Don't expose yourself to this kind of scrutiny unless you sound/look or appear credible under pressure

Nuance-focused questions

Few of us are as precise in our use of language as we should be. We allow clichés and catch-phrases to replace carefully considered comment. Public sector mission statements are full of such things. They will cheerfully talk about *empowering people* or *building capacity* or *enabling change* or whatever. Frequently these buzz words are drawn from government documents and speeches. The *Third Way* could be described as a haven for such imprecision.

Now in the day to day bustle of bureaucratic life, these gems can be very helpful. They can help you to get things done. Not long ago local government managers inserted the words *best value* into just about every public statement - *we are refocusing our services in line with the outcome of our recent best value review.* Health is no different. There are smatterings of *patient involvements, modernisations* and *choices* all over the place. Schools talk about educating the *whole pupil* or *providing a holistic educational experience.*

Councils parade *cradle to grave services.* And everyone is involved in *partnerships, joint-working* and *being joined-up.*

The truth is that this stuff is currency in public sector corridors. But it doesn't always bear close scrutiny under questioning.

Nuanced-focused approaches are underpinned by one key question:

What exactly did you mean by...?

For interviewees, this question can be hell on earth. So used are we to imprecision and being able to get away with buzz words that when we are closely questioned it can put us on the back foot.

For example:

Q: *You've recently carried out a best value review of your crematorium services?*

A: *Yes, that's right. We believe we've got a better focused approach to meeting the whole needs of families and communities.*

Q: *What exactly do you mean by their whole needs?*

A: *Yes, we set up a focus group of local families and community members to find out what they think of our services and we believe we better meet their whole needs.*

Q: *What, in the crematorium service?*

A: *Yes, it's critical we provide a holistic service.*

Q: *Not really, surely. You cremate the dead.*

A: *Yes. But there's more to it than that.*

Q: *Yes. Your review made that clear - you charge them more to cremate their dead.*

A: *Our revised charges are in line with the council's best value charging policy review.*

Q: *How does charging people more to cremate their dead relatives meet their whole needs - when what you are doing is taking away more of their money?*

A: *We are working hard in partnership with local people to meet their whole needs.*

Q: *You've cut back your services, revised your charges and you're cremating their late relatives at higher rates than you did a year ago - that's the reality isn't it?*

How to deal with nuance-focused questions:

▲ Be clear about your message

▲ Word it in plain English

▲ Look at how it might be challenged or interpreted

▲ Don't use jargon

▲ Don't use buzz words or fillers

▲ Challenge yourself before anyone else does - what are you really saying?

▲ And if you're forced to go into uncomfortable territory, don't change horses - stick to your line

Common sense questions

These questions cut through jargon and professional explanation since they start from what *the man in the street* might say. Common sense can be quite seductive. So in a broadcast interview, for example, where it could be put to you that *most people might think this or that* it can be harder to argue the contrary.

Listen out for phrases in questions which suggest what people might think. And if you can, argue your point on the basis of the facts of an issue rather than what might be argued as prejudices or accepted truths. Equally, you can use common sense to turn the questions back on the interviewer.

Here's an example:

Q: *You've recently agreed to put up the allowances given to councillors. The leader of the council now earns upwards of £40,000 a year. Most people might think that a great deal of money for a job that until a couple of years ago would have been done for next to nothing.*

A: *And that's the problem. Most people don't understand what councils actually do. The fact is that the leader of the council is responsible for a budget of over £400 million. Most of us would expect a company director responsible for that kind of budget to earn a lot more than £40,000 a year. A recent survey by the CBI showed that the average salary for a director of a medium sized company is around £100,000 a year.*

Q: *That may well be the case. But there is a difference: companies pay their salaries out of profit; councils pay their salaries out of tax. Most of us would say they are quite different.*

A: *And we would agree with that. Most of us would probably accept that companies produce things we might want - with one or two exceptions - whereas councils manage services that most of us need - schools for our children, care services for our elderly relatives, road sweeping and refuse collection for our homes. Most of us would miss those things more than we might miss a new car or a better kitchen.*

And so on.

Assertive questions

Sometimes a journalist will simply want to put a proposition to an interviewee and effectively dare them to accept it or deny it. This is a more combative approach and fairly similar to the kinds of things we might hear in court when a prosecuting barrister starts to interrogate a witness.

Interviews can get fairly heated at such times, although quiet persistence can be equally effective. Whichever, it's really important that the interviewee maintains his or her control and does not deviate from the message that they were intending to convey anyway.

Q: *It is the case, is it not, that these restructuring proposals are badly thought through, ill-considered and politically expedient?*

If you don't agree with the assertion, don't agree with it. State your key message even though it may not be a direct answer to the question.

A: *Let me be clear: the council is considering a series of organisational options which will mean better services, brighter futures for local people and a better value bottom line.*

Recap or summary questions

Sometimes in the midst of an interview we may be tempted to blind the interviewer with science. We will present our world as a very complex place and describe it in jargon and specialised language. It may, if that is our intention, throw a journalist of the trail of the story that he or she might be following.

But this technique can easily be dealt with by the journalist by presenting back to the interviewee a version of what he or she said in simpler language. This can work brilliantly on the air since listeners can be quickly lost by jargon and the journalist will appear to be helping to make sense of complexity. In truth, that is what they are in all likelihood doing.

It presents a challenge for the interviewee since the interpretation of what they are saying can stand in for what they actually said. On the air, we, as listeners, can easily be convinced that the *interpreted* comments represent what the interviewee was *actually saying* - only they couldn't quite get it out. In print, paraphrased comments can become, to all intents and purposes, what the interviewee said.

Unfortunately, there can be a massive gap between what you, as the interviewee, appeared to say, and what you meant.

It would work this way:

Q: *Is it likely that hospital waiting lists will be cut significantly this year?*

A: *It's difficult to predict at this stage because we are working our way through the changes in policy at this moment and there are some complex staffing issues which will need to be resolved before we can publish our estimates - we wouldn't want to pre-empt those discussions.*

Q: *So what you're really saying is that awkward staff are getting in the way of cuts in waiting times.*

Actually, it's not what the person said at all. But unless that interpretation is challenged then it could quickly become the case. If we heard it on the air and were not convinced by a robust rebuttal we may believe it to be the case.

A soft rebuttal might be:

A: *I wouldn't want to pre-empt discussions. Staffing matters are complex.*

Listeners might well think that the journalist had it right the first time.

A harder rebuttal would be:

A: *No, that is not what I'm saying at all. These are complex matters and it helps no-one to over-simplify them. What I am saying is: It's difficult to predict at this stage because we are working our way through the changes in policy at this moment and there are some complex staffing issues which will need to be resolved before we can publish our estimates - we wouldn't want to pre-empt those discussions.*

The re-affirmation may not be sexy - it's not the best sound-bite in the world - but if it's what you wanted to say then you would have to make sure that you drove the point home.

Possibility questions

Journalists use a number of questions to invite you to concede the possibility of something. The fact is that many things are possible; the question that should concern you is whether they are likely. You should be careful of possibility questions.

▲ Is there a danger?

▲ Is it not possible that...?

▲ It sounds to me that what you're really saying is...

The difficulty with possibility questions is in avoiding the temptation to make unforced concessions. Most things are possible but it doesn't mean that any of those possibilities should be confirmed. Imagine the chaos that would ensue if certain key people confirmed possibilities.

Question to an airline pilot: *Most people accept that the skies are getting busy to the point of extreme congestion. Is it possible that there could be a multiple aircraft collision over London?*

A: *That is possible and certainly we are concerned about the number of planes in the skies over London.*

This could become: *An airline pilot today predicted that a multiple plane collision over London is possible.*

Bob Smithson said: *"We are concerned about the number of planes in the skies over London".*

The general guide here is: unless you want the possibility to be confirmed as your key message then don't make the concession.

Question to an airline pilot: *Most people accept that the skies are getting busy to the point of extreme congestion. It sounds to me that what you're really saying is that there could be a multiple aircraft collision over London?*

A: *No. I don't see that as a problem at all. While there are more planes in the skies than there were ten years ago our skies have never been safer - we have made massive improvements in air traffic control. It's safer in the skies than it is on 99% of British roads.*

Be clear about what you want to say and don't make any concessions that you don't have to.

People tell me...
One questioning technique is where the journalist may suggest that they

have been told something already by someone else. It may be a source inside your organisation. It may be an outside source. Or it may, and this is what you have to watch, be no one at all. The journalist may simply be flying a kite to see what kind of reaction the question gets.

The trouble is that this questioning technique can very quickly put us on the back foot. And particularly so if the question seems to be informed - we may hear words, phrases or assertions that we know others have used.

From an interviewing point of view it's possible to speculate about what people may or may not have been saying. Common sense alone will tell an interviewer that, for example, if you are cutting services some people will be unhappy, others will think it's politically motivated, others still may believe that someone is settlings personal scores and so on. And each or all of these assertions may be true. But unless you planned to share your whys and wherefores with the world then don't allow yourself to be tempted.

Once again you need to stick to your key message. Spending time anticipating possible questions will help you to feel more secure. But deviate and you could quickly find yourself lost in detail that you had not planned to share.

Stupidity and flattery

Journalists don't always present themselves totally honestly. Nobody does. That's not to say they will lie. Rather, they may pretend to be something that they are not. One technique that they can use is to pretend to be stupid. If they can convince the interviewee that they really don't know what he or she is talking about, that they simply don't understand, then the interviewee might begin to simplify the message to get their point across.

But more, when we believe another person to be stupid we can all start to patronise or make other assumptions about this person's intelligence. The net result can all too easily be that we let our guard down. From an interviewing point of view this is very powerful stuff since the interviewee can be lured into territory they had not planned to visit or into making statements that are over-general.

Here's an example:

Q: *You've had a lot of adverts for Accident and Emergency staff recently. Is it hard to get doctors?*

A: *Getting suitably qualified A&E consultants is a challenge to our trust. We set high standards and we want to maintain them.*

Q: *That's really surprising. I mean, they're really well-paid jobs aren't they?*

A: *It's not a question of money alone.*

Q: *How do you mean - they might not want to work in this area - it's nice here, I've lived here all my life.*

A: *Hmm.*

Q: *It seems a nice place it really does - the doctors look as though they get on really well.*

A: *Well, they don't always but that's life.*

Q: *Tell me about it. It's like that at our place - talk about stress.*

A: *Stress is a factor here. I think A&E consultants are getting picky about the kinds of places they'll work. It can be quite stressful here. Our staffing has been cut in recent years.*

Behold, the guard is down and the interviewee has now made a number of unforced concessions. What started out as one message about standards - *Getting suitably qualified A&E consultants is a challenge to our trust. We set high standards and we want to maintain them* - turns into a different kind of story altogether.

Here's what it looks like:

- ▲ There have been budget cuts

- ▲ Stress may be a factor in recruiting A&E consultants

- ▲ And a quote: "I think A&E consultants are getting picky about the kinds of places they'll work. It can be quite stressful here. Our staffing has been cut in recent years."

Flattery is usually there for a purpose

Journalists may also use flattery to get us to lower our guard. For some strange reason we are frequently tempted by those who flatter us. Look out for the warning signs:

- ▲ Thanks for seeing me, I know how busy you are - *you are a very important person*

- ▲ I don't know how you keep tabs on all of this it's so complicated - *you are very intelligent, much more so than I am*

- ▲ I've been very keen to meet you for ages - *your reputation precedes you, you are well known*

Whenever you encounter flattery in the midst of an interview, assume that it's there for a reason. If it's not and you genuinely are a wonderful person put the compliments under your belt and get on with the job. Otherwise ignore it.

Watch how the hardened manager softens and makes unforced errors.

Q: *So does this new report mean that the council is likely to cut back on any services?*

A: *It's not as simple as that - there's a long consultation process which we are obliged by law to go through.*

Q: *We never consult anyone - we just publish and get on with it. It must be really hard to keep control of all of that stuff.*

A: *Well, we're pretty organised. We have people who do these things.*

Q: *All the same, I'm always taken aback when I realise just how complicated things in councils are. I think my job's a lot simpler.*

A: *It can get pretty complicated. But we do our best.*

Q: *So all these groups that you have to consult - must be a bit of a bind, what with so many other things to do.*

A: *It can be - sometimes we can guess what they might say in advance.*

Q: *Really, is it predictable - I wouldn't know how people might think - I guess you get a pretty good feel for how people are likely to think. It's about experience I guess.*

A: *Yeah, absolutely. Community groups are the worst - if they don't get what they want through the consultation then they usually go bleating to councillors...*

I exaggerate for effect - no-one is going to be that silly - but this kind of thing does happen. The net result is a corking quote - *community groups are the worst - if they don't get what they want through the consultation then they usually go bleating to councillors...* - and a story that can be milked ad infinitum.

Watching the detectives - the Columbo

The Columbo is named after the famous TV detective who was known for asking questions when suspects least expected it. In fact it's no fiction. Erving Goffman, the American sociologist showed that we are more likely to believe passing or unintended remarks than deliberate comments.

When you consider that so far as the journalist is concerned the interview might begin the minute you meet and not finish until they physically leave you, there's a lot of time when you might respond *off the cuff* to incidental questions.

In reality, the Columbo has become a key part of public life. Many organisations rely upon this kind of technique in their recruitment processes. What, if not this, are *informal opportunities for a drink with some colleagues?*

The key point here is not to lower your guard at any point. Anything you say at any point could and will be used if it's interesting.

Here's the end of an interview. See how easily the journalist slips the Columbo in.

Q: *So thanks, that was really interesting. And you'll be sending through the press release?*

(Journalist packs away the tape recorder and notebook and stands up.)

A: *Yes, I'll get Sarah, our Press Officer onto it straight away.*

Q: *Oh yes, I know Sarah. She's pretty on the ball.*

(Journalist slips on her coat and heads towards the door.)

A: *She's been a great find, Sarah.*

Q: *So it was really nice to meet you.*

(Journalist opens the door.)

Q: *Goodness I almost forgot, there was one thing I meant to ask you...*

(Journalist turns round and looks scatty.)

Q: *...what was it now? (Pause.) Is it likely that you'll be making these cuts before Easter...?*

And then the journalist will wait and hope for an unforced error. Sometimes it will work, sometimes not. But it's often worth a try.

Under pressure

Some interviewers will keep pushing you until the pressure shows. It can happen fairly quickly when you're in unfamiliar surroundings, such as a radio interview. The key for the journalist is not to push you so far that the audience sympathises with the interviewee who is clearly getting a battering.

The fact is that when we are under pressure we will start to experience a *fight or flight* response. We'll either panic and want to be out as soon as possible or we'll gear up for the challenge itself.

You should be aware that it's quite normal to feel panicky under pressure. You will recognise it as your heart starts to race, your skin starts to sweat and you will feel a little out of control. In these circumstances, it's easy to allow yourself to give ground.

Don't. Never change horses in mid-stream.

Imagine your Director of Human Resources has agreed to give an interview on a damaging school inspection. If your position is *we have looked closely at the report and realise that there are many lessons we must learn and quickly,* you will not look very sensible if you suddenly start apportioning blame.

It can happen. Your Director of Human Resources might agree to do an interview on radio to talk about lessons from inspections. It sounds like a good way of stressing the *we are only human* element in your learning message. And then faced with some difficult questions might make unplanned concessions.

Interviewer: *Would you say that you have learned lessons from this inspection?*

Director of HR: *Absolutely. The thing about an inspection is that it gives you an opportunity to look at your own performance and to take stock. I have to say that we have looked closely at the*

> *report and realise that there are many lessons we must learn and quickly.*

I: *You've been there a while...*

DHR: *I'm sorry?*

I: *You've worked with the council for some time haven't you?*

DHR: *Yes, I've been with the city council for about 20 years, man and boy as they say.*

I: *You must have seen it coming surely. You've probably seen all this stuff before?*

DHR: *I think we've learned a great deal...*

I: *Oh come on, let's be honest, there's nothing in this report that a good HR director wouldn't have seen coming a mile off.*

DHR: *Of course, we always have our performance under review.*

I: *Which is to say that you saw this coming a mile off...*

DHR: *I wouldn't go that far....*

I: *How far would you go?*

And then your Director of Human Resources is on the defensive, presumably feeling a bit battered and glad to make the concessions so that it will all go away. Except that it won't.

No comment

Don't assume that simply saying *no comment* will kill a story. It may lead to the statement *senior managers refused to comment*. Always think about how it will look or sound to the audience.

16 Making your service media-safe

Who's in charge?

Be clear about who is overseeing your media operation. If it's a senior officer who is not communications-trained, ensure that they are well-advised. A natural caution might limit your organisation's ability to get the most out of media relations. Equally, a communications officer may not be able to command the respect needed by senior managers.

Who's allowed to speak, who's not?

Be clear about who is licensed to talk to the media. Some organisations build this into their staff contract. There is no question that poorly handled media relations can adversely impact on your organisation's reputation. So you need to be clear about who will speak and on what basis they will be selected. You should also ensure that they are able to muster the appropriate skills. It does no harm to have a clear policy that says staff need a special dispensation to talk to the media - that removes any doubt. Don't forget that journalists like to talk to the people who do the job.

What are they going to say and do they know it?

You should have processes for agreeing the way in which messages are going to be built. Ideally, these should be linked into either your media strategy or your communication strategy or both. If you find yourself scrabbling around to put together a message for an interview you probably shouldn't be doing the thing in the first place. Keep focused on the main point - outcome, audience, message.

Can you get coordinated?

If yours is a big organisation you will need to think about how you coordinate your media relations. Look at what you send out from the point of view of the local media. It can be all too easy to swamp the local news desk with releases from different parts of the same organisation. That doesn't say that you're media-savvy - it says that you're disorganised and chaotic. And that's not a good message to send out.

Where and who are the leaks likely to come from?

Where there are opportunities to use the media for mischief or personal gains there will be leaks. Keep a tight rein on the *version control* of your documents - this can make it easier to track leaks. Be wary of widely circulating important material by email. If leaking is a problem, you can always resort to verbal briefings and withdrawing documents after meetings. But it's practically impossible to stop leaks altogether. There may be times when you will want to use this method yourself to get key but unattributable messages out.

How will you plan?

Think about how you will link your business or corporate strategy and your media activity. As is suggested elsewhere in this booklet, the two should be closely linked. You will encounter Enthusiasts who will want to take any and all opportunities to get your organisation into print and they may come armed with the proposition that *all publicity is good publicity*. That's only a phrase and you shouldn't run your communication strategy off the back of a cliché.

How will you review?

You should have procedures in place whereby you can capture and review the media coverage you get. Some organisations use press clipping services. Others do this themselves. Some record everything that is broadcast. If you are going to be able to improve your media management you need to be able to review the coverage you get, and, equally importantly, the stuff you manage to keep out of the media.

Are you clear about the right skills being in the right place?

Broadly speaking, you will need credible people who are capable of delivering a message irrespective of the pressure they may be put under. Importantly, they may not fully believe the message themselves. But that may not actually matter - they still need to be capable of putting it across as though they do. That's not to say that they will be expected to lie. But they may be expected not to give their personal opinion.

Training

We're all so used to being a part of the media experience - we listen daily to people getting grilled - it's easy to start imagining that dealing with journalists is easy. It's not.

Just as this was going to press James Naughtie, from Radio Four's flagship programme Today, accused one interviewee of coming from the planet Venus. It was a tough and probing interview on the future of the Conservative Party. The interviewee fared well. But he might easily have folded under the pressure.

If you are preparing for a major interview make sure that you get someone who understands the media machine to put you through your paces. An ex-journalist would be a good place to start. Be challenged. Find your weaknesses. Feel the heat.

The truth might well be that you are simply not comfortable in a challenging interview environment. If so, it's a lot better to find that out before you get anywhere near the media. If it happens - and it does - on live radio it's not just your reputation that gets affected. Someone who falters in an interview will cause their organisation to be seen differently. If you are asked questions to which the audience believe you should know the answer and you're found wanting that could well raise even bigger questions about organisational competence.

In the final analysis, you must never lose sight of the fact that although it's unfair that we get judged by the image we present through the media, it is what happens. And rightly or wrongly, media management skills are as important today as meeting management skills were yesterday.

Press Complaints Commission Code of Practice

The Press Complaints Commission is charged with enforcing the following Code of Practice which was framed by the newspaper and periodical industry and ratified by the Press Complaints Commission, 19th March 2003:

All members of the press have a duty to maintain the highest professional and ethical standards. This code sets the benchmark for those standards. It both protects the rights of the individual and upholds the public's right to know. The Code is the cornerstone of the system of self-regulation to which the industry has made a binding commitment. Editors and publishers must ensure that the Code is observed rigorously not only by their staff but also by anyone who contributes to their publications.

It is essential to the workings of an agreed code that it be honoured not only to the letter but in the full spirit. The Code should not be interpreted so narrowly as to compromise its commitment to respect the rights of the individual, nor so broadly that it prevents publication in the public interest.

It is the responsibility of editors to co-operate with the PCC as swiftly as possible in the resolution of complaints.

Any publication which is criticised by the PCC under one of the following clauses must print the adjudication which follows in full and with due prominence.

1 Accuracy

i) Newspapers and periodicals should take care not to publish inaccurate, misleading or distorted material including pictures.

ii) Whenever it is recognised that a significant inaccuracy, misleading statement or distorted report has been published, it should be corrected promptly and with due prominence.

iii) An apology must be published whenever appropriate.

iv) Newspapers, whilst free to be partisan, must distinguish clearly between comment, conjecture and fact.

v) A newspaper or periodical must report fairly and accurately the outcome of an action for defamation to which it has been a party.

2 *Opportunity to reply*

A fair opportunity for reply to inaccuracies must be given to individuals or organisations when reasonably called for.

3 **Privacy*

i) Everyone is entitled to respect for his or her private and family life, home, health and correspondence. A publication will be expected to justify intrusions into any individual's private life without consent

ii) The use of long lens photography to take pictures of people in private places without their consent is unacceptable.

Note - Private places are public or private property where there is a reasonable expectation of privacy.

4 **Harassment*

i) Journalists and photographers must neither obtain nor seek to obtain information or pictures through intimidation, harassment or persistent pursuit.

ii) They must not photograph individuals in private places (as defined by the note to clause 3) without their consent; must not persist in telephoning, questioning, pursuing or photographing individuals after having been asked to desist; must not remain on their property after having been asked to leave and must not follow them.

iii) Editors must ensure that those working for them comply with these requirements and must not publish material from other sources which does not meet these requirements.

5 Intrusion into grief or shock

In cases involving personal grief or shock, enquiries should be carried out and approaches made with sympathy and discretion. Publication must be handled sensitively at such times but this should not be interpreted as restricting the right to report judicial proceedings.

6 *Children

i) Young people should be free to complete their time at school without unnecessary intrusion.

ii) Journalists must not interview or photograph a child under the age of 16 on subjects involving the welfare of the child or any other child in the absence of or without the consent of a parent or other adult who is responsible for the children.

iii) Pupils must not be approached or photographed while at school without the permission of the school authorities.

iv) There must be no payment to minors for material involving the welfare of children nor payments to parents or guardians for material about their children or wards unless it is demonstrably in the child's interest.

v) Where material about the private life of a child is published, there must be justification for publication other than the fame, notoriety or position of his or her parents or guardian.

7 *Children in sex cases

1. The press must not, even where the law does not prohibit it, identify children under the age of 16 who are involved in cases concerning sexual offences, whether as victims or as witnesses.

2. In any press report of a case involving a sexual offence against a child -

i) The child must not be identified.

ii) The adult may be identified.

iii) The word "incest" must not be used where a child victim might be identified.

iv) Care must be taken that nothing in the report implies the relationship between the accused and the child.

8 *Listening devices

Journalists must not obtain or publish material obtained by using clandestine listening devices or by intercepting private telephone conversations.

9 *Hospitals

i) Journalists or photographers making enquiries at hospitals or similar institutions should identify themselves to a responsible executive and obtain permission before entering non-public areas.

ii) The restrictions on intruding into privacy are particularly relevant to enquiries about individuals in hospitals or similar institutions.

10 *Reporting of crime

(i) The press must avoid identifying relatives or friends of persons convicted or accused of crime without their consent.

(ii) Particular regard should be paid to the potentially vulnerable position of children who are witnesses to, or victims of, crime. This should not be interpreted as restricting the right to report judicial proceedings.

11 *Misrepresentation

i) Journalists must not generally obtain or seek to obtain information or pictures through misrepresentation or subterfuge.

ii) Documents or photographs should be removed only with the consent of the owner.

iii) Subterfuge can be justified only in the public interest and only when material cannot be obtained by any other means.

12 Victims of sexual assault

The press must not identify victims of sexual assault or publish material likely to contribute to such identification unless there is adequate justification and, by law, they are free to do so.

13 Discrimination

i) The press must avoid prejudicial or pejorative reference to a person's race, colour, religion, sex or sexual orientation or to any physical or mental illness or disability.

ii) It must avoid publishing details of a person's race, colour, religion, sexual orientation, physical or mental illness or disability unless these are directly relevant to the story.

14 Financial journalism

i) Even where the law does not prohibit it, journalists must not use for their own profit financial information they receive in advance of its general publication, nor should they pass such information to others.

ii) They must not write about shares or securities in whose performance they know that they or their close families have a significant financial interest without disclosing the interest to the editor or financial editor.

iii) They must not buy or sell, either directly or through nominees or agents, shares or securities about which they have written recently or about which they intend to write in the near future.

15 Confidential sources

Journalists have a moral obligation to protect confidential sources of information.

16 Witness payments in criminal trials

i) No payment or offer of payment to a witness - or any person who may reasonably be expected to be called as a witness - should be made in any case once proceedings are active as defined by the Contempt of Court Act 1981.

This prohibition lasts until the suspect has been freed unconditionally by police without charge or bail or the proceedings are otherwise discontinued; or has entered a guilty plea to the court; or, in the event of a not guilty plea, the court has announced its verdict.

*ii) Where proceedings are not yet active but are likely and foreseeable, editors must not make or offer payment to any person who may reasonably be expected to be called·as a witness, unless the information concerned ought demonstrably to be published in the public interest and there is an over-riding need to make or promise payment for this to be done; and all reasonable steps have been taken to ensure no financial dealings influence the evidence those witnesses give. In no circumstances should such payment be conditional on the outcome of a trial.

*iii) Any payment or offer of payment made to a person later cited to give evidence in proceedings must be disclosed to the prosecution and defence. The witness must be advised of this requirement.

17 Payment to criminals

Payment or offers of payment for stories, pictures or information, must not be made directly or through agents to convicted or confessed criminals or to their associates - who may include family, friends and colleagues - except where the material concerned ought to be published in the public interest and payment is necessary for this to be done.

The public interest

*There may be exceptions to the clauses marked * where they can be demonstrated to be in the public interest.*

1. The public interest includes:
i) Detecting or exposing crime or a serious misdemeanour.

ii) Protecting public health and safety.

iii) Preventing the public from being misled by some statement or action of an individual or organisation.

2. In any case where the public interest is invoked, the Press Complaints Commission will require a full explanation by the editor demonstrating how the public interest was served.

3. There is a public interest in freedom of expression itself. The Commission will therefore have regard to the extent to which material has, or is about to, become available to the public.

4. In cases involving children editors must demonstrate an exceptional public interest to over-ride the normally paramount interest of the child.

Reproduced with permission from the Press Complaints Commission.

About reputation

Reputation is a strategic communications consultancy working across the public sector. To find out more visit www.e-reputation.co.uk. Or phone 0870 902 0907.